THE GREAT BLACK SWAMP

THE GREAT BLACK SWAMP

TOXIC ALGAE, TOXIC RELATIONSHIPS, AND THE MOST INTERESTING PLACE IN AMERICA THAT NOBODY'S EVER HEARD OF

PATRICK WENSINK

Belt Publishing

First Edition 2025
ISBN: 9781540270108

Belt Publishing

www.beltpublishing.com

Cover by David Wilson

For my parents, Ron and Deb

CONTENTS

PART I

The future of life on Earth depends on our ability to see the sacred where others see only the common.

—John Denver

1
A SHRUG, AND A SMILE, AND BACK TO NORMAL

The only way to truly understand Northwest Ohio, and Lake Erie's toxic algae problem, and the region's secret history as a bloodthirsty, uninhabitable swamp that was once home to the worst road in America is to first go through John Denver. Specifically, how in 1973, the city of Toledo pretty much issued a fatwa against the gentle, squeaky-clean folk singer who, seemingly, had nothing to do with the place.

The year 1973 was an optimistic one when good-time movies like *The Sting* topped the box office; it was the year Tony Orlando and Dawn had a number-one hit with their wholesome "Tie a Yellow Ribbon Round the Ole Oak Tree"; the year silly, yet wonderful, things like garlic knots and the band KISS were invented, both in Queens, New York; and the year of the Paris Peace Accord, which essentially ended the Vietnam War.

How was this also the year that lovable, boyish John Denver became Northwest Ohio's public enemy number one? Maybe because 1973 was also a complicated year. A dark, paranoid year. It was the year Americans were so edgy that *Tonight Show* host Johnny Carson accidentally created a nationwide toilet paper shortage just by making a single joke; the year the Watergate Commission was established and eventually led to President Richard Nixon's resignation; and the year actor Bruce Lee mysteriously died. It was such a tumultuous year that scandals even plagued the International Soap Box Derby World Championship across the state in Akron, where fourteen-year-old winner Jimmy Gronen was found to have cheated by installing an electromagnet in the nose of his racer.

So, this was a time and a place when harmless John Denver could conceivably be threatened with violence by a medium-sized American city. There's light and dark in Northwest Ohio. Good and evil. Villains and heroes. Often all so tightly woven together, like some kind of Midwestern double helix, that you'd probably never even notice.

But Denver was supposed to transcend light and darkness. He was an artist perfectly positioned to rise above the chaos of 1973. The elfin, bespectacled musician was blossoming into a megastar that year, thanks to his upbeat hit song "Rocky Mountain High." John Denver was, perhaps, the one person that both grandparents and hippies might conceivably enjoy together. This affable, golden-haired golden child was meant to bring us together again.

And yet, Toledo's mayor, Harry Kessler, hated Denver with a fist-pounding fury, saying publicly: "Boy, am I going singe him. I'll send that son-of-a-gun a letter he'll never forget."

One *Toledo Blade* reporter took it further, calling Denver a "demon-eyed, furtive-browed, nothing-is-sacred pop singer." That writer, Tom Gearheart, added, "Somebody had better warn Denver before he ambles into Toledo, June 16, that instead of a key to the city, he may just be handed a live grenade."

What had captured the town's anger? Recently, John Denver had performed a song on Carson's *Tonight Show* titled "Saturday Night in Toledo, Ohio."

"That song is offensive as hell to me, and I'm sure it is to the people of this city," Mayor Kessler added. "It's disgraceful."

Lou Thompson, head of the Labor Management Citizens Committee—a man who also once coauthored a scorching letter to Gloria Steinem after the feminist icon said Toledo, her childhood home, was rat-infested—called Denver's tune "a dastardly lie" and said he'd like to take the singer on a tour of the city some Saturday night, "to the places my wife doesn't know about."

Denver's TV performance had whipped everyone into a frenzy by committing the unforgivable sin of calling the forty-seventh-largest city in America *boring*. "Saturday night in Toledo, Ohio, is like being nowhere at all," the song begins, featuring just Denver's honey-sweet voice and an acoustic guitar. "Saturday Night" was a staple of his live act, but it had never been beamed out to twenty million people for a laugh until now.

The rest of the lyrics don't make Toledo look much better. For roughly two and a half minutes, Denver's angelic lyrics emphasize how the most interesting things to do here are watch the grass die, stare at buns rising at the bakery, or weigh yourself on one of the city's famed scales. That last part was probably the only passage citizens and civic leaders didn't find offensive. Toledo was, in fact, the scale-manufacturing capital of the world at the time. From factory floors to doctors' offices to delicatessens, if you saw a device meant to weigh something or someone, it probably had the name TOLEDO boldly emblazoned on it. People in town were proud of that. It was the kind of hardworking, blue-collar, practical manufacturing that this place was built on.

Amid the controversy, Denver canceled that June performance. He suspiciously claimed television commitments in London were the reason, but he did reschedule the concert for November.

"Last time you were here," Johnny Carson said a few months after the initial broadcast, "you did a song about Toledo, right?"

"Yep," Denver replied, nodding a little bashfully. The troubadour wore his signature wire-rimmed granny glasses beneath a blond pageboy haircut. His skinny legs were poured into black trousers, and he wore a maroon paisley shirt, with a gold medallion around his neck.

"We heard from a few people in Toledo," Carson cracked. The host was decked out like a groovy JCPenney suit advertisement from the era. "It was kind of a good-natured rib, right?"

"Oh yeah, it's a satirical kinda song," Denver said in the gee-whiz way America would come to recognize from concert stages and Muppets specials for decades to come.

"What were some of the lyrics in that song?" Carson said, tossing a perfect comedic softball to the diminutive singer.

"Saturday night in Toledo, Ohio, is like being nowhere at all." Denver recited the opening line flatly, as if reading a statement in court, almost like he was a little hesitant to possibly work up anyone's ire again. "And it goes on from there."

Carson paused a beat, probably assuming there'd be an outpouring of laughter. Instead, the silence was interrupted by only a few weak, awkward chuckles from the crowd. Ever the pro, the host shifted gears away from Northwest Ohio to Denver's recent marriage, and the folk music everyman shared a raunchy anecdote about making so much love on his honeymoon that his wife cracked a rib. To which Dom DeLuise, Denver's neighbor on the couch, held up the singer's arm like a prizefighter.

Several months later, toward the end of autumn in 1973, when the leaves were stripped from the trees and Lake Erie's cold wind started to barrel through town, John Denver finally played Toledo. On a Saturday night, of course. If he had disrespected a larger city like Miami or San Francisco, I wouldn't be shocked to learn that vinyl albums were piled up tall and burned, tickets ripped up en masse, or maybe even that a riot broke out. Not two years earlier, the Newport Jazz Festival experienced a riot during a Dionne Warwick performance, so marshmallowy soft concerts like this had the potential for violence in a strange year like 1973.

However, Denver's reception took a decidedly Northwest Ohio turn.

"For a no-account slanderer, John Denver is disgustingly pleasant and easy to talk with," wrote Gearheart, *The Blade* reporter who was once filled with so much bile he was ready to hand the singer an explosive device. Even though Denver was recording an album in New York, the singer took time to speak with Gearheart. "He said that he performs 'Saturday Night' early in the show to loosen the audience, and they usually respond with belly laughs."

When the city's blood pressure finally lowered, Northwest Ohio suddenly shared those laughs. Editorials flooded the newspaper, demanding that the mayor get a sense of humor about the whole thing, and others declared that, you know, Toledo *was* boring, and they liked it that way. In fact, maybe Denver wasn't even the one to be mad at, since "Saturday Night in Toledo, Ohio" was actually penned by the New Christy Minstrels' Randy Sparks. "I suppose Randy was on the road, travelling around, and wanted to write a song to express a feeling about some towns on a bad day," Denver told *The Blade*. "It's really less about Toledo than about all the seemingly boring places people go to. Why Toledo? Well, Toledo sounds better than Fargo."

Denver performed for over six thousand people at the city's largest venue, the Toledo Sports Arena, and the entire town seemed to have dealt with the awkwardness of getting national attention for all the wrong reasons with surprising grace. Instead of holding onto that anger when things got difficult and weird, Toledo caught a serious case of Denver Fever.

"'This song is the greatest thing for our city that's ever been done,' Merle Gore beamed with unabashed enthusiasm," *The Blade* said upon Denver's arrival. Gore, the manager of the Toledo Area Convention Bureau, made the singer an honorary member of the group. "To which Denver replied, 'Far out.'"

A civic welcome wagon presented the singer with everything but a key to the city, including a yellow pullover saying "John Denver is strong for Toledo"; a music box that played the city's anthem, "We're Strong for Toledo"; a newspaper cartoon depicting Denver playing his guitar while the mayor and others carry buckets of tar and feathers; and, curiously, a tie clip, cuff links, a tape measure, and a desk pen set from the Toledo Scale Company, which included the note, "Thanks for the plug."

"[Denver's] public relations agent, Lee Solters, walked away from the reception shaking his head," Gearheart wrote. "'I'm not putting you on....This is the most friendly bunch of people I've ever met, and I travel all over the country. But more important, the people here give a damn about their city and that's something you just don't see very often.'"

› › › › › › ›

I spent the first eighteen years of my life in Northwest Ohio and never heard so much as a peep about this John Denver fiasco. I can't remember seeing anything that has made this particular pocket of the Midwest get so angry before or since. It's honestly kind of surprising. But the fact that this explosive reaction was swept under the rug is not a surprise.

This seems to have been treated as an anomaly.

A crop circle of emotion.

We do not tend to wear our feelings or our history on our sleeves in Northwest Ohio. In fact, this whole John Denver controversy is, oddly, a good example of a way of thinking that has shaped the region for the last two hundred years. Whenever things get heated, or difficult, or weird, we don't tend to lash out—instead, we shrug, and smile, and go back to normal. Or at least tell ourselves everything's normal. And things have definitely gotten difficult and weird here. Whether it's taming the most uninhabitable land in America; literary icons trash-talking us long before Denver was even born; arson rings; John Dillinger's buried treasure; or a scandalous president using a Northwest Ohio teen to vault himself into the White House, we've responded in that same ambivalent manner. Though we almost never threaten to hand someone a live grenade anymore, we often shrug, we smile, and we get back to normal. Myself included. It's not only a pragmatic, friendly way to live but also one that can have awful repercussions. Take, for example, the weirdest, most difficult moment of all: that time in 2014 when Lake Erie turned to neon-green cyanide and almost killed four hundred thousand people in Toledo.

PART II

All Americans come from Ohio originally, if only briefly.

—Dawn Powell

2
THE WATER WASN'T EVEN LIKE WATER ANYMORE

It's never been easy being Ohio, nor has it ever been easy being from Ohio.

There often feels like a distinct lack of respect out there in the rest of the world. It can often feel like the whole planet thinks the same way author Bill Bryson does, who warned readers in one of his popular travelogues: "You are going to have a day without even the tiniest of pleasures; you are going to drive across Ohio." No matter where I am, this kind of thinking seems to permeate. The mention of being an Ohioan has never once elicited excitement or curiosity in others, unless that other person was also from Ohio. It's easy to feel like Ohio has become the middle child of America. It seems that a majority of people think we are not as sophisticated and historic as all those East Coast states, yet not as flashy as those West Coast states. It's easy to see why, what with our distinct lack of snow-capped mountains or tech hubs or Siegfried and Roy performances. According to a recent *U.S. News & World Report* poll, Ohio only ranks number one in a single category: affordability.

We don't, frankly, do ourselves many favors selling the sizzle. Like how if you squint at a map, the state is kind of shaped like a heart, so from 1984 to 2001 and, oddly, again in 2023, the state's Division of Travel and Tourism slapped everything with the slogan "Ohio: The Heart of It All." Other than pointing out that our borders kind of look a Valentine's card, the catchphrase tells outsiders absolutely nothing about the place. Which is about right, since the only other category we'd rank number one in is "not drawing attention to ourselves."

But I have a confession.

I love Ohio.

Specifically, I love the part where I was raised—the heart's upper left atrium. Even more precisely, that rural part about an hour outside of Toledo. An area that is, most likely, the state's least-known region. Northwest Ohio's population density is so low, and its land so empty, that even other Ohioans look down on it as something like narcolepsy in geographic form. In college, my friends, all from metropolitan parts of the state, lightheartedly nicknamed me the Hillbilly, even though I defended myself by pointing out, "The joke's on you. We don't *have* hills."

A writer once said Northwest Ohio is so empty and flat he could spot another car's headlights from twenty miles away. This region mainly consists of one million acres of cornfields and wheat fields and soybean fields. Farmland so level that as a boy I couldn't find a place to sled on when it snowed. There are no capital-C cities here, except for Toledo, a name the rest of the nation might not ever even utter if not for the phrase "Holy Toledo." Northwest Ohio is almost completely composed of towns whose populations are often smaller than most urban high schools. I grew up in one of them, a two-stoplight working-class farming village called Deshler, with a population in my childhood that tipped just below two thousand depending on how many people died or went away to college that year.

Today, it's early June, and I am back in Deshler. I'm visiting my parents for a week, and this morning I have decided to see some toxic green algae. That means I have to head toward Toledo.

Currently, I'm a college professor in the Appalachian Mountains of Tennessee and don't get home very often. But when I do, I luxuriate in driving everywhere. When I'm behind the wheel in Northwest Ohio, I'm almost always overcome by a sense of peace and bigness. Sure, you might be able to see another set of headlights twenty miles away while driving down these needle-straight rural roads, but that's a good thing because that also means you are being cradled by a limitless blue sky and soft clouds. All that flatness and emptiness creates a panorama effect that feels warmly inviting; it slows my nerves.

I have barely begun my drive this morning and immediately notice that all the ditches are filled to their tops with water after a serious rainstorm. That runoff and I have formed an unlikely tag team this morning, since we both have the same destination: Lake Erie. We both begin around Deshler's table-flat farmland, zigzagging in identical northeasterly paths along small state highways. I'm in a struggling 2010 silver Hyundai speckled with dents and missing a passenger-side door handle. The car has a leak in the trunk, so the interior traps some serious mustiness after a rain. My son often calls it "The Fartmobile" when it smells like it does today.

That iced tea–colored water flows alongside the roadway in intensely deep, V-shaped earthen ditches. These gulches are everywhere in Northwest Ohio and, as I remember one high school teacher boasting, nowhere else on Earth. I recall that teacher saying with pride that these enormous raw soil trenches are our region's defining geographic trait. In Northwest Ohio, wherever there is a rural road, you are almost guaranteed to find a deep drainage ditch running parallel. As one Federal Works Project writer poetically noted in a Depression-era Ohio travel guide, these neatly packed rows of drainage "run across the fields like strings on a harp." This morning, those harp strings are filled to capacity because the dense clay soil refuses to absorb much rainwater. And there's a lot of water. An average ditch is about fifteen feet wide and probably almost ten feet deep, and they often run unbroken into the horizon. This morning, all twenty-five thousand miles of ditches in Northwest Ohio seem like they are on the verge of overflowing, as if nature is aching to flood this place again and turn it back into a swamp.

I woke up early so I could beat the heat. But the June sun is already so bold and powerful I'm squinting through sunglasses as I drive toward Toledo. The AC is blasting, which is no small feat for this weary car. The Hyundai is also so old it still has a CD player—and I am so old I still own CDs. So, on this trip home I've vowed to listen only to the original CDs from my teen years growing up here—Nirvana, Black Flag, Sonic Youth, the Jesus Lizard, Pavement, L7, the Breeders. Awkward music for an awkward kid; out-of-tune instruments for someone who felt equally out of tune with Northwest Ohio in the 1990s. A lonely kid who spent a lot of time out on these lonely roads, just driving and thinking and driving.

The coffee my dad made hasn't fully kicked in, and it feels too early for all that screaming punk noise, so I try to wake up by listening to

NPR. The news claims that today is the hottest non-summer day in Toledo history as I whip past stubby green fields that only come up to your waist. In another couple months, this corn will be taller than a basketball hoop, and with it will come the unique fear of tall corn tightly lining both sides of the backroads. Mothers will tell children never to play in the fields, whispering stories about getting lost and cries for help going unheard because of the densely packed stalks. At dusk and dawn, every driver will get a little edgy, knowing that at any second a leaping deer could blindly burst from the corn and instantly be in front of your speeding car. According to the Ohio State Highway Patrol, almost 110,000 car accidents involving a deer have occurred in the last five years alone, with nearly 50 being fatal. Two Northwest Ohio counties rank among the top four in the state in terms of these accidents.

But there is a beauty to these fields, too, especially when they are just sprouting like this. There's a geometry I love about corn. It's planted with a precision and intentionality I cannot attain in my own life lately. These exacting rows stretch into the horizon, like they were cut by laser. As a boy riding in the back seat of our van, I'd do that Magic Eye–poster focus at those perfect rows buzzing past at fifty-five miles per hour until a vibrant optical illusion formed, looking almost like a sprinting green set of legs in a flip book.

I sneak a peek out the Hyundai's window and am instantly brought back to that time—a much happier time when I was little—and it puts a smile on my face.

For the hourlong drive to the lake, it's almost all farmland and frothy ditches until the very fringe of Toledo, where my travel buddy merges with hundreds, maybe thousands, of other ditches and blends into the Maumee River. The relatively short 137-mile river is fed by over 3,900 miles of rivers, creeks, and ditches.

The Maumee River continues to skim right alongside me, running parallel to Front Street. Together, we buzz by the recently built Hollywood Casino and past the massive PBF Energy refinery, which produces 180,000 barrels of gasoline, diesel, nonene, xylene, tetramer, and toluene per day. Farther down Front Street, we are dwarfed by the clinically white, skyscraper-tall Mondelez grain silos, home to the second-largest flour mill in the country. A few stoplights beyond is the Saint Mary's Cement terminal and the Heidtman Steel Foundry. The river's coastline is dotted with a mix of rusted barges and operational ones. The water veers away from me right where the Maumee dumps into Lake Erie. It's here that the road takes a sharp right curve, away from the coastline. This road next leads into the suburb of Oregon (pronounced "ore-uh-GONE"), where I pass the former BP Oil refinery, which was purchased by Cenovus Energy in 2023, a sprawling lakefront campus of fire-breathing pipes and white storage domes that looks like an alien moon base and produces 160,000 barrels of gasoline per day. Across the street is the Oregon Clean Energy Center, which is the first time I've laughed all morning. My joy gets doused on realizing this is not an office of environmental do-gooders pitting themselves against the mega petroleum producer but a cleverly named power plant that runs on fracked natural gas.

Mercifully, a bright spot arrives as I pass the headquarters of 104.7 WIOT-FM, my favorite classic rock radio station as a teen. They did not play Sonic Youth or Jesus Lizard; nobody did around here. That was something I listened to in secret. One of many such things I did in secret. But when I was not listening to punk albums, I also gobbled down a steady diet of 104.7 fist-pumpers by Led Zepplin and Heart. Normal music.

Almost like "The Home of Nonstop Rock and Bob and Tom in the Mornings" was some gateway to nature, the industrial smokestacks vanish and the landscape returns to the gentle countryside I left back in Deshler. It is peaceful and open except for the dozens of steel electrical transmission towers with swooping black power lines, likely from the nearby Davis-Besse Nuclear Power Station. Another sharp left reveals Maumee Bay State Park's dense green tree canopy bursting upward against the surrounding farm fields. This is a gem of the state parks system—well maintained, loved, and lush. Its 1,300 acres seem to be a magnet for bird-watchers, who have been known to camp several nights to get a glimpse of some of the three hundred species passing through here. It claims to be the warbler capital of America, a fascinating natural distinction that was also never shared with me growing up here.

I follow signs toward the beach and instantly recognize it from all the 2014 news footage of the Toledo algae crisis, hoping to maybe see a toxic bloom today. There is not a bloom, though, because it's too early in the season. Instead, the water looks pretty normal. But there's no mistaking its checkered past. Several billboard-sized signs are planted right up against the gently lapping shore, promising that toxic algae* is always a possibility.

* Author's note: I treat *algae* as an uncountable or mass noun, like politics, and thus use singular verbs and pronouns with it throughout the book.

BE ALERT! AVOID WATER THAT:

- Looks like spilled paint.
- Has surface scums, mats, or films.
- Is discolored or has colored streaks.
- Has green globs floating below the surface.

AVOID SWALLOWING LAKE WATER.

Below these warnings are eight images of various kinds of waterborne funk and deformity, each about as pleasant as an autopsy photo. They each look like something you could have easily found on that balmy day in August 2014, back when Lake Erie was suddenly so thick you could pick it up and eat it.

That would've been suicidal, but you could have.

Up close, the water back then was as deep green as the Chicago River on St. Patrick's Day. From farther away, it was something else entirely. From newscopter footage, it actually looked sort of beautiful if you accidentally walked into the room and didn't know what you were watching. On that day, August 2, 2014, Lake Erie looked like a poetic curl of clashing greens from one hundred feet up. A swirling pattern almost exactly like a slab of marble. Maybe Verde Alpi, the finest Italian marble, cut from the Western Alps, prized for its complexity and flow—famous for that deep olive background interlaced with kiwi-colored waves all sloshing together like a twenty-million-year-old lava lamp.

The focal point of all these national news shots of the lake were those kiwi-green tendrils, which mysteriously stretched from the shore to almost a dozen miles out. Right about where the city's drinking water intake was. But the cameras always panned up for shock value, because directly behind this mutant water was downtown Toledo, a modest cluster of tall office buildings only about as high up as the helicopter itself.

"I went out last night; you could hear the wash of the waves, and what I saw was putty. Literally green putty," naturalist Sandy Bihn told a radio station. "The water wasn't even like water anymore."

In only about a day, Toledo's pebbled coastline had become covered in a thick, viscous Gak tangled with bloated fish. Dog owners were warned not to let their pets drink it. Several TV reporters took the opportunity to hold up a glass and compare it to some expensive kale-rich health shake.

This strange, lime-colored goo was actually an algae bloom so large reporters said it was visible from space. A bloom so toxic it could have killed the entire city, around four hundred thousand people, in a matter of days thanks to those drinking water intakes. Chances of death were, thankfully, low, but it had been known to happen. It was all probably pretty confusing, since the tap water looked clear and normal. However, the Environmental Protection Agency warned that, if ingested, the toxins would most likely cause nausea, vomiting, diarrhea, severe headaches, fever, and even organ damage. The EPA told residents: don't drink it, don't brush your teeth with it, and boiling it only makes it stronger. One scientist claimed that downing a single glass could send your body into complete liver failure. Public events were canceled and restaurants closed their doors. Hospitals rescheduled elective surgeries and sent instruments to other cities for disinfection. Toledo issued a DO NOT DRINK ordinance on everything dripping from its pipes. Bottled water became a commodity about as rare as Italian marble. Panic levels rose so high Mayor Michael Collins compared this emergency to 9/11. Wisely, he later apologized, but this overreaction speaks to the depth of fear hitting Toledoans when they looked out at one of the largest freshwater basins on Earth and found a 260-trillion-gallon margarita that was, according to one scientist, "more toxic than cyanide."

Today, I stand on the water's edge and think Lake Erie could be an ocean. It has an endless horizon that frames more of that wide-screen sky I saw on my drive up here. Blue as a sapphire, the sky's reflection marries with the calm brown water and becomes the spitting image of the Atlantic. The lake seems huge, and it's unthinkable that Canada is only sixty miles from this small beach.

Though it is not the narrowest Great Lake—Lake Ontario beats it with a mere width of fifty-three miles—Erie is the shallowest by a huge margin, only 210 feet at its deepest spot. For context, nearby amusement park Cedar Point currently has six roller coasters taller than that—its Top Thrill Dragster doubling Erie with its 420-foot drop. This shallowness has led to Erie's rapid warming in recent years. Those other, deeper Great Lakes have also seen an increase in temperature, but nothing like Erie.

A barely perceptible breeze carries the nautical smell of fishy decay and mildew. White strands of cottonwood fluff swirl through the breeze, like someone blew a thousand dandelions. Delicate, long mayflies attach themselves to my shirt. It's calm and quiet and lovely; just looking around here, I'd say Lake Erie has made a beautiful recovery from its cyanide tap water days.

A couple families splash around the water, and children shout with joy as they dive after a frisbee. A few young women lie motionless on brightly colored towels, soaking in the blistering early morning sunrays. Others walk along the cusp of the lake or sit in steel porch swings facing the horizon. It's only 9:30 a.m., and my forehead is glistening with sweat and coconut-scented sunscreen.

"Go ahead, jump in!" someone calls. I see a white-haired couple rocking gently in a swing. The woman smiles and motions toward the softly lapping waves.

"I think I'm a little overdressed for the beach today." Ever the contrarian, I decided to wear jeans and sneakers and a gray button-up even though I knew it would be broiling hot.

"You could just take your shoes off!"

"I think I'll pass." I look back at the water and wipe my forehead. Cooling off sounds great, but then I see the toxic algae warning signs again and remember the industrial nightmare I drove past just to get here. "Hey, can I ask you both a question?"

3

A TOWN TOO TOUGH FOR TOXIC WATER

Toledo was born with its back to the wall in 1837, along the absolute western fringe of American civilization at the time. To skim the surface of the city's early history is to read about countless battles with the British and Native tribes. It is also a sad example of manipulative agreements with those Natives, like the Treaty of Greenville that pushed tribes farther west or deeper into the uninhabitable Great Black Swamp. Battle after battle, followed by a seemingly endless string of lopsided diplomacy.

The earliest accounts of the city reflect these darker times. Take Methodist preacher Joseph Cross, who wrote: "Of all the towns I ever saw, I think [Toledo] is the most miserable. The place is so sickly that few will consent to stay here, except blacklegs and desperadoes."

That outlaw reputation slowly faded in favor of something recognizably normal and Midwestern. But for a hot minute, Toledo had a chance to be something spectacular. Hopes were so high that in 1878, newspaper publisher J. W. Scott wrote an enthusiastic seventy-page pamphlet that would have made John Denver do a spit take. It was called *Future Great City of the World* and predicted that within one hundred years—ending, essentially, the year I would be born—Toledo would surpass London and New York as the center of global commerce. Surprisingly, Scott wasn't a crackpot. The pieces for success really did start to formalize: Toledo had hardworking citizens, a thriving manufacturing sector, and most importantly, it became a logistical unicorn. By the mid-1900s, several interstates crossed paths there, it was flush with train yards sending goods in all cardinal directions, and it had a thriving port that was only a short trip across Lake Erie, up the St. Lawrence Seaway, and out to the Atlantic and a lucrative global economy.

Toledo, for a variety of reasons, never grabbed its brass ring the way other Midwestern cities like Chicago did. Instead of becoming a future great city, it settled for just being a future normal city. But it still hung on to a little desperado swagger. By the 1940s, Toledo had become the illegal gambling capital of America, packed to the gills with underground casinos. According to casino historian John Scarne, Club Devon once housed the largest number of illegal gambling tables in America. In fact, the saying "Holy Toledo" originated with mobsters in nearby cities like Detroit and Cleveland, who found that the city's police looked the other way at their illicit activities and thus considered it a sanctuary city.

This exciting information, too, was not shared with me as a boy. Even though I went through a brief phase when I thought John Gotti was the most interesting person on Earth.

The next time Toledo became nationally noteworthy, about the time J.W. Scott had it scheduled to body slam New York and London for global superiority, was the 1970s: weirdly, Toledo's pop-culture decade. The city not only had John Denver dunking on it in front of millions of TV viewers, but it also pinged cultural radars via George Carlin's marijuana-saturated comedy album *Toledo Window Box* and Kenny Rogers's heartbreaking 1978 Grammy-nominated song "Lucille," which is set in Toledo. But the highest-profile Toledo moment of the decade came courtesy of actor Jamie Farr's role as Corporal Klinger on *M*A*S*H*. Farr, who was born in Toledo in 1934, had Klinger tout Toledo's virtues each week, such as Mudhens baseball and Tony Packo's hot dogs. The plot of one episode actually revolves around a shortage of blood bags in the operating room, so the gang uses Packo's sausage casings for transfusions. Farr's delightful pride in his real-life hometown pulled double duty as a legitimate love letter to this city but could also seem like a bumpkin joke. Whether intentionally or not, Farr promoted Toledo to the world as somehow both normal and weird.

Today, the city doesn't get a lot of attention by most big-time tourism standards. It has no Instagram-ready regional cuisine, unless Michelin stars are awarded for sheer volume. (At Tony Packo's, the cashier dismissed me with a sharp eyeroll after I declined to add a chili dog to my enormous plate of chicken paprikash and homemade dumplings.) Because it has no mountains or National Parks, its lone natural distinction is Lake Erie. The city's architecture is orderly and all fairly recent, reflecting the twentieth-century industrial boom when it cranked out more Toledo Scales, Jeeps, and windowpanes than anyone. It has a modest university, a very nice art museum, and a zoo that gets national praise. It has one of those phantom downtowns that seems completely empty unless the Mudhens are playing a home game. The bulk of the Maumee River's waterfront is lined with vacant factories leftover from that manufacturing gravy train.

Much like John Denver's publicist noted in 1973, Toledoans love this place and have, in fact, come to relish its underdog status. The city prides itself on that most Midwestern of civic virtues: avoiding flash in favor of stability. Or as cultural critic P.J. O'Rourke noted about his hometown in a 2014 opinion piece written at the height of the algae crisis, Toledo is "America's friendliest junkyard." But as the crisis continued, its citizens didn't flinch. Toledo proved it was, as O'Rourke added, "a town too tough for toxic water."

During the algae crisis, experts began explaining that the danger within Lake Erie's new Mountain Dew complexion was not exactly the algae but more specifically the microcystin in cyanobacteria. What is commonly known as blue-green algae is actually cyanobacteria, and the microcystin contained in it is a toxin so poisonous that if more than one part per billion is detected in water, it's unsafe to drink. That's the equivalent of one drop of water in an Olympic-sized swimming pool. Toledo's water registered 2.5 parts per billion, nearly triple what the World Health Organization classified as safe.

So, while *algae* is not the scientifically preferred term, it's the one most popularly used for this phenomenon, and it is the one we'll be using from here on out. Sorry, scientists.

As August's heat rose, so did the anxieties of a thirsty city. It was unclear how long the tap water would remain poisonous, and citizens began stockpiling anything drinkable. "My sister woke me up at 6:00 a.m. saying that people are starting to run out to the stores and hoard water," said one local newspaper reporter on the first day of the "Do Not Drink" ordinance. Lines formed around the block at groceries, convenience stores, and anywhere that might conceivably sell water. "It looked like Black Friday," one woman said at a pharmacy. By 9:00 a.m., one shopper described Costco as a war zone. People were seen on the side of the road hawking Dasani for twenty-five dollars a case.

This shocking change was understandably making citizens quite angry. "Can't wash dishes, can't wash up, can't cook," one woman told the *CBS Evening News*. "It's hell."

By Sunday, Toledo had been without water for forty-eight hours with no end in sight. Civic leaders' requests for patience felt infuriatingly weak, to say the least. "I want to make sure that I would be comfortable with my family—my daughters and my wife—drinking the water," Governor John Kasich said after declaring a state of emergency.

Would people begin dying of dehydration? Would hospitals buckle after hundreds or even thousands of desperate Toledoans tried to stay alive by drinking tainted water? Would the city descend into civil unrest? All possibilities were on the table, and none were good.

As the grip of the crisis squeezed tighter, and things got heated and difficult and weird, that Northwest Ohio friendliness poured in from every conceivable angle. A nearby Anheuser-Busch brewery began delivering aluminum cans full of clean drinking water. The National Guard hauled in enormous thirty-thousand-gallon tanks of potable water, from which folks filled up everything from old bottles to Tupperware to beer growlers and coffee pots. Farmers dispensed hundreds of gallons of clean water from their wells. Some Toledoans traveled great distances, like schoolteacher Katie Peters, who drove an hour to a Michigan Walmart in order to stock up on bottled water for her neighbors. "Our community has really come together," she said.

Though police officers were posted outside grocery stores as shelves emptied, the city never fully embraced its anger and didn't descend into chaos. Instead, tough Toledoans shrugged and smiled through awful circumstances and then got back to normal.

By mid-Sunday, these water delivery methods were working, and nobody had died as a direct result of the toxic water. This moment of relief gave folks enough pause to ask some questions they were too panicked to consider over the last two days.

"What people are wondering is when did city officials know? When did the numbers spike on the water?" asked *Toledo Blade* reporter Marlene Harris-Taylor.

City leaders from top to bottom claimed to have been blindsided by the toxins. "This is Mother Nature we're dealing with," Water Commissioner Ed Moore said. "This is beyond our control. There is nothing we could have possibly done different to prevent this."

However, *The Wall Street Journal* quickly uncovered documents that gave Mother Nature a solid alibi. Apparently, the Ohio Environmental Protection Agency sent a letter to the mayor nearly two months earlier, pleading: "I cannot underscore boldly enough the precarious condition of Toledo's drinking water system and the imminent vulnerability to failure."

Quickly, every news outlet in the country established a foothold in Toledo, broadcasting those Verde Alpi helicopter shots and those kale shake images along Toledo's man-made beach, and reporters pulled out their thesauruses, comparing this deadly water to pea soup, pond scum, and even the Wicked Witch of the West's skin.

By Sunday evening, as the workweek approached, a new worry had entered the picture. It was a pain to bathe and brush and wash dishes without tap water, but at least the vast majority of the population was healthy for now. They must have wondered, *How long will this last?* Surely, images of Flint flashed through their heads. The infamous Michigan city one hundred miles north had its own crisis only five months earlier due to lead in its water supply. Flint was just beginning to understand the long-term effects of toxic water consumption, especially on the health of its children, and the outlook was dark. *Are we next?* Toledoans must have asked, using Aquafina to boil their kids' macaroni on Sunday evening.

While the public began asking questions and looking for a villain, the city spent over $4 million neutralizing the toxins with a mix of aluminum and chlorine. This shock to Lake Erie's system worked. On Monday morning, Mayor Collins hoisted up a clean, clear glass for reporters. "Our water is safe," he said, taking a swig. "Here's to you, Toledo. You did a great job."

He was right. It was a miracle nothing worse happened. Toledoans were unable to drink tap water for three days, which is about the limit a human body can handle without water before organ failure and eventually death occur. The *Columbus Dispatch* reported sixty-nine people visited hospitals fearing they'd fallen ill, but it could have been so much higher. It's terrifying to think about what could have happened to homeless populations, the elderly, and others without the means to secure clean water if this crisis continued even one day longer. The fact that every citizen was cared for is a testament to the first responders, civic leaders, grassroots organizers, and the toughness of Toledo. Not an ideal solution, but one that solved the problem. Finally, the crisis was over. The preceding three days had been a test for the residents of Toledo. It seemed like a moment the city would never forget.

4

THE MOST INTENSELY CULTIVATED REGION IN THE STATE

"Hey, can I ask you both a question?" I say to the man and woman on Lake Erie's shore on this blazingly hot June day.

Their grins vanish, probably expecting a speech on how to get into heaven or a request for a dollar. My Midwestern politeness recoils at making anyone uncomfortable, so I quickly ask if they were in Toledo back in 2014 and what they remember about the algae scare.

"There wasn't much swimming then," the man says, chuckling. His name is Les. He's a pot-bellied retiree wearing mirrored shades and an Air Force ballcap.

His wife, Pam, is good-natured, curly-haired, and staring happily at me through huge glasses. They tell me they met when Les was a country and western line dance instructor. He surprises me by saying he is actually familiar with Deshler because he once taught at The Bavarian Haus, a polka music hall decorated in what you could describe as "cuckoo-clock chic."

Les and Pam didn't actually see the algae in person and weren't too worried about it back then. Les has a theory about the green toxins being a byproduct of the nuclear power plant. "Oh yeah. They were pouring shit in there."

"Then they put a no-no to it," Pam adds.

I've never read anything about nuclear waste on Lake Erie, and I tell them I was under the impression the harmful green algae stemmed from other, more innocent sources. Les and Pam disagree, but politely.

We chat a little more about their kids, and I say I must be off to the state park's other main attraction, the Trautman Nature Preserve. Supposedly, it offers an untouched parcel of the Great Black Swamp, which is exciting because I'd heard the swamp had been wiped off the map.

They wish me good luck, and I leave them in the searing heat, merrily swinging on the shore with a view of the billboard warning against toxic algae. I begin to wonder about what other Toledoans recall from that horrific time, now almost a decade later.

The Trautman Nature Preserve visitor's center is about the closest thing we have to a Great Black Swamp museum, and I am instantly in love. Taxidermied wolves and hawks sit atop display cases stuffed with historic artifacts. The walls are lined with photos and maps detailing that long-vanished wetland. My eye catches a chart displaying all the native animals that have gone extinct here. According to the chart, each disappeared from this area during the last quarter of the 1800s, exactly the time humans started the nearly impossible task of settling this land. Almost exactly the time my great-great-great grandfather Henry planted his first field outside of Deshler.

The extinct animals include:

- River otter
- Wild turkey
- Porcupine
- Timber wolf
- Mountain lion
- Beaver
- Bison
- Grouse

- Black bear
- Lynx
- Wolverine
- Elk
- Passenger pigeon

Ohio has a strange relationship to the passenger pigeon, a sleek creature that used to be the most abundant bird in the world. So abundant that John James Audubon once observed a continuous migration of passenger pigeons in nearby Kentucky that he claimed darkened the skies for three days. In 1855, three Ohio men reportedly netted 1,800 passenger pigeons in a single night. The last documented wild passenger pigeon on Earth was shot in Pike County, Ohio, in 1900; "Martha," the last living passenger pigeon of any kind, domestic or wild, died in the Cincinnati Zoo in 1914. In roughly a century, passenger pigeons went from an estimated population of 5 billion to total extinction; in that same span, the forest cover of the state went from nearly 100 percent to about 10 percent. A major part of that deforestation was centered on Northwest Ohio.

A plaque on the wall reads: "The Great Black Swamp that was Northwest Ohio's last wilderness was completely transformed from a swamp forest into the most intensely cultivated region in the state." This sign sits beside a hexagonal clay tube, a drainage tile from the 1880s. Millions of these little clay pipes were sunk under the soil to drain the swamp. This older version, and today's drainage tile made from long, corrugated plastic piping, are a miracle to farmers because they prevent fields from flooding by funneling all that rain into all those ditches I followed to get here this morning.

Enthused by swamp history, I eagerly head outside toward the wetland nature preserve to catch a glimpse of the remains of the Great Black Swamp.

"Watch out for scat," a smiling woman says as we pass in opposite directions on the thin boardwalk. I thank her and step carefully around black nuggets of poop, too small to be a dog's and too big to be a rodent's. Wolf, maybe? What does wolf poop even look like?

The Black Swamp was once deeply feared for its wolves. Also, it was legendary for its seemingly bottomless mud. I look down and see that the water here is covered in a mix of lime green scum and itty-bitty lily-pad-looking things, a few of which are blooming white. It's exactly how I think a swamp is supposed to look somewhere like Florida or Louisiana, places chock-full of alligators and fan boats. The air is filled with the sounds of bullfrogs groaning like someone abusing a cello and also an odd, more chaotic noise in the distance. Something mechanical and violent—construction happening just beyond the tree line.

My enthusiasm doesn't last as I start to put the pieces together.

I do that a lot—get swept away in a moment and lose all critical thinking. Yes, Trautman has wild animal scat, and deep water, and some mysterious wetland scuzz—but it's not the horror movie Black Swamp I've heard so much about. This is not a place of misery, unless you count the brutal sunlight cooking my flesh, which is what brings me back to reality. The Trautman Nature Center's wetland area is missing the Great Black Swamp's famously dense tree coverage. Supposedly, it was so thick with trees that it was pitch black, even during the daylight. There is almost no tree canopy here. Instead, it looks like a graveyard of bony dead stumps poking up from the slime. It's as if the old Great Black Swamp has been hit by a bomb. The grinding, growling noise of construction equipment only adds to that sad vibe.

"All the ash trees are gone because of emerald ash borer, and what replaced them was silver and red maples. That impacted the high and low water cycles," a park ranger tells me. "You should be able to go out into the marshes like ours and walk on the land in the summertime. It should be dry out there. And that hasn't happened for like six years." Apparently, all that standing water knocked out the maple trees, which accounts for this apocalyptic landscape.

I walk on and begin to sweat. Tall plants that look like saw grass wave in the gentle breeze. The ranger tells me that these are phragmites, which are an invasive species that filled the void once the ash and maple trees all died out. These harmless-looking blades of grass are anything but harmless because they reduce plant diversity, which reduces animal diversity. Before you know it, the whole ecosystem is collapsing, and when the natural ecosystem collapses, the lake starts trying to kill people.

My chance to see a fragment of the swamp has been dashed, so I decide to track down more firsthand accounts of the 2014 algae crisis. Les and Pam admitted that they weren't witnesses, so I get an urge to poke around town, find real Toledoans and hear real horror stories. I ask the ranger in the visitor's center, and she tells me she wasn't here in 2014, but her husband was. "I know he only drinks bottled water now," she says.

Not exactly the spine-chiller I anticipated, but it's a start. Plucking off skinny black mayflies, I jump back in my sweaty Hyundai and set off looking for more tales of deadly algae.

5

HAVE YOU THANKED A CYANOBACTERIA TODAY?

Deadly algae problems are nothing new to humanity. One *Scientific American* article, "Toxic Slime Contributed to Earth's Worst Mass Extinction—And It's Making a Comeback," points out that stuff like this has actually been mopping the floor with living creatures for eons. Some 252 million years ago, Earth experienced what is called the "Great Dying" when wildfires, drought, and rapidly warming oceans killed off 70 percent of land species and 80 percent of aquatic species. "We also found that algae and bacteria had proliferated soon after the extinction, infesting freshwater ecosystems with noxious slime," says the article. Sounds unimaginable, right? "In fact," it notes, "they reached concentrations typical of modern microbial blooms, such as the record-breaking blooms in Lake Erie in 2011 and 2014."

Lake Erie had, in fact, gone green with algae before, and actually, 2015's bloom was far larger. However, none threatened as many lives as 2014's water crisis.

Dr. Greg Boyer, the director of the Great Lakes Research Consortium and emeritus professor of biochemistry at SUNY

College of Environmental Science and Forestry, says we need to look back to the Mayans to understand the power of algae today and its threat to our future. "While we are a bit more advanced than the Mayans in terms of water quality, our demands on water resources are constantly increasing, at the same time that our insults to those water resources are equally increasing." He refers me to a paper that outlines how the ingestion of microcystin-infected water likely weakened the Mayans and led to their eventual defeat as New World explorers brought violence, disease, and repression.

Those looking for more examples don't need to go back to the dawn of time, or even a distant civilization. Whether you realize it or not, toxic algae is currently all around us and getting worse. "Toledo's fertilizer-haunted water supply is hardly an isolated case," agricultural writer and researcher Tom Philpott says. One article states "the US National Office for Harmful Algal Blooms estimates that the blooms cost the nation upwards of $50 million annually in costs related to health, fisheries, recreation, tourism and monitoring. A 2017 survey of nearly 1,200 US lakes revealed that about a third of the lakes contained cyanobacterial toxins," one article states. "And that number is growing." The EPA reported fifteen thousand bodies of water with algae-like nutrient problems in 2023, and all fifty states have had a toxic algae outbreak, and usually more than one. Harmful algal blooms have been reported on every continent but Antarctica. *Scientific American* noted that in the last two decades, algal blooms have increased in size by about 13 percent worldwide, which means if you cobbled them all together the blob would take up about as many square miles as the entire nation of India. According to the latest National Oceanic and Atmospheric Administration (NOAA) projections, the Gulf of Mexico is home to one of the largest algae blooms on Earth, and this year's version will be just average in size—blotting out sea life for 5,400 square miles, roughly the same size as Connecticut.

It's not just the size of these dangerous green mats that has folks worried, because the impact of this algae is being felt in life-threatening ways. Yes, drinking water supplies around the globe are at constant risk the way Toledo's was. But there was also the small city in Brazil where over fifty people died in a medical facility that was accidentally treating patients with microcystin-infected IV fluids. There was the family and their dog who were recently found dead on a hiking trail in Yellowstone after swimming in a algae-laced creek. And three hundred endangered elephants in Botswana died after drinking from algae-plagued puddles.

So, while it's easy to see that it's been around forever, and is deadly, and is probably in my backyard, it's still not so easy to understand *what* this algae is. According to NOAA:

> Ranging from microscopic, single-celled organisms to large seaweeds, algae are simple plants that form the base of food webs. Sometimes, however, their roles are more sinister. Under the right conditions, algae may grow out of control—and a few of these "blooms" produce toxins that can kill fish, mammals and birds, and may cause human illness or even death in extreme cases. Other algae are nontoxic, but eat up all of the oxygen in the water as they decay, clog the gills of fish and invertebrates, or smother corals and submerged

> aquatic vegetation. Still others discolor water, form huge, smelly piles on beaches or contaminate drinking water. Collectively, these events are called harmful algal blooms, or HABs.

The cyanobacterial toxins in HABs are what make them so dangerous, and they are fascinating. Scientists like Bowling Green State University's Dr. George Bullerjahn have dedicated whole careers to this strange little quirk of nature. "Everybody thinks cyanobacteria are bad guys because they cause these blooms. Actually, they make about a third of the oxygen in the atmosphere, mostly in the ocean. And there are plenty of good-guy cyanobacteria doing their business every single day, too," Bullerjahn, professor and director of NIEHS/NSF Great Lakes Center for Fresh Waters and Human Health, tells me. "Remember that old bumper sticker: HAVE YOU THANKED A GREEN PLANT TODAY? You can also thank some cyanobacteria."

So cyanobacteria is simultaneously the thing that almost killed four hundred thousand people in Toledo and the thing that fills our atmosphere with oxygen. This is not a simple Western movie with a good guy in a white hat and a bad guy in a black hat. Everyone's wearing gray, or maybe green?

The rising number of HAB events around the globe has people like me worried about what the future will look like if we don't find a solution.

"Civilization will go on, but with serious consequences," says Bullerjahn. "Safe water will become more scarce, affecting vulnerable populations in developing countries and the poorer regions of wealthier countries. That means water is more expensive, food will become more expensive due to scarcity of irrigation water and reduced fisheries from large lakes."

These disruptions are becoming more and more obvious already, including the aforementioned death toll of humans in Brazil and Yellowstone. But animal life currently seems most vulnerable, and the scale is far scarier than the tragic death of those African elephants. For instance, the Audubon Society claims that algae killed ten thousand fish in Oakland's Lake Merrit in 2022, which they estimate will likely lead to thousands of migrating birds starving to death, which will cause more food chain chaos that will slowly work its way back to humans. The Gulf of Finland recently turned neon green, killing a shocking number of animals, which led to water scares similar to Toledo's. A recurring Florida algae bloom known as the "Red Tide" killed hundreds of sea turtles, dolphins, and manatees. Domestic animals, like dogs, have proven to be so greatly at risk that *Outside* magazine recently issued a guide to identifying algae to keep humans and pets safe while on walks and hikes near bodies of fresh water.

Undrinkable water, animals dying, people dying. It all starts to sound like Armageddon. As Greg Boyer notes, it's not the *end* of the world, but it puts us several ticks closer. "As water becomes more scarce, vulnerable populations will migrate to more favorable locations. That will result in political unrest, conflict, and worse."

NOAA ecologist and Lake Erie HAB expert Dr. Reagan Errera adds, "The thing that keeps me up at night is the bloom hiding under the ice in Alaska. Once that melts, the results will be catastrophic."

So, while Lake Erie's 2014 outbreak was far from the first harmful algae bloom on record, it seems to be the first domino that captured the twenty-first-century public's attention. And things seem to be getting worse by the day. It makes you wonder, why don't we just fix the problem?

For starters, the cause of bright green murder algae is not exactly what you might think. When I started digging, I assumed, much like Pam and Les, that one-hundred-gallon drums stenciled with radioactive symbols were spilling Day-Glo ooze into our waterways. But that is nowhere near accurate. Instead, toxicity has a lot more to do with places like the extinct Great Black Swamp and something that has been right under my nose my entire life.

Most toxic things, I will discover, look pretty normal until they're not.

6

ORVILLE REDENBACHER, WE HAVE A PROBLEM

A few days after the 2014 Toledo algae crisis ended, people were relieved to drink their tap water again, but they still needed to know: How did this happen? An answer quickly emerged, and suddenly, remote places like my microscopic hometown came under fire.

"Toledo sits on the Maumee River, which flows into Lake Erie and carries with it chemical leachings from the corn and soybean fields that dominate the river's 8,300-square-mile watershed," noted the Natural Resources Defense Council. "Principal among those chemicals is phosphorus, the fertilizer ingredient that nourishes blue-green algae and promotes toxic algal blooms whenever the conditions are right."

And if you guessed conditions were right in August 2014, you win a kale-green health shake.

A US Department of Agriculture's Natural Resource Conservation Service study estimated that 80 percent of the phosphorus was from commercial fertilizer found in those endless, laser-straight farm fields now inhabiting the former Great Black Swamp. You could almost hear politicians and news cycles breathing a sigh of relief. Finally, the Toledo algae crisis had a villain. The practice of farming was quickly made out to be a sin on the level of sneaking razor blades into Halloween candy.

The enemy was suddenly anyone busting ass from dawn to dusk producing the food that made the world go around. Articles often gave the vibe that agricultural professionals were some sort of tractor-driving war criminals. Very rarely would they credit these same people for producing the goods that put food in our stomachs, fed our animals, and even powered our cars.

This strikes me as deeply problematic for another reason. Almost every farmer I've ever known from Northwest Ohio is kind, hardworking, and decent. I make jokes and criticize the area, but at their core these are good people. Not villains. Yet the fact remained that actions in their fields were primarily to blame for a lake being poisoned and hundreds of thousands of people almost dying in Toledo.

Can someone be guilty and innocent? Be kind but still cause such destruction?

"The problem isn't farmers," Don Scavia, a researcher with the University of Michigan's Graham Sustainability Institute and one of the few voices defending agriculture back in 2014, said. "The problem is farm policy. We're just overwhelming the system by the number of acres we're planting with industrial corn."

Corn?

Steaming yellow ears stacked up high on the dinner table. Tortillas. Frosted Flakes. Bags of Orville Redenbacher. How could all those yummy kernels be the source of green lake scum? Back in 2014, the average person probably never found out because the media's fascination with toxic algae quickly lost traction. More than likely, attention shifted because when we stop blaming farmers and start blaming breakfast cereal and popcorn and the things we feed our livestock, the villain of this story starts looking like someone very familiar. The bad guy is suddenly standing in our mirror.

Corn is everywhere, and we as consumers in twenty-first-century America have an insatiable appetite for it. In 2023, the USDA reported that ninety million acres of corn had been planted, so if America's cornfields were a country, it would be roughly between the size of Japan and Germany. According to the *Washington Post*, "Today, the United States is the largest producer and consumer of corn—and by a long shot. Corn is in the sodas Americans drink and the potato chips they snack on; it's in hamburgers and french fries, sauces and salad dressings, baked goods, breakfast cereals," as well as just about any meat you can imagine. "The grain is so ubiquitous that it would take longer to list the foods that contain traces of it than to pinpoint the ones that don't." In fact, about 75 percent of all processed food in the United States contains corn.

However, less than 10 percent of that corn is directly ingested by humans, says reporter Roberto Ferdman. "The bulk is either turned into ethanol, for use as fuel, or fed to the hundreds of millions of animals we raise. Cows, chickens, pigs and even fish, which are fed pellets made largely of corn, eat several times the amount of the grain consumed by people each year."

Corn is among the neediest crops when it comes to fertilizers, the Canadian Broadcast Company pointed out. "In fact, there's so much corn being farmed in some parts of the region that it's not possible to deliver the amount of fertilizer they require in the spring. There just isn't enough rail cars to do that."

It didn't take much sleuthing to connect this obsession with corn to a 2013 study that noted a 218 percent increase in phosphorus loadings in the Maumee River over the years leading up to the algae crisis. The same study shows a 42 percent increase in runoff during the same span. Those deep, V-shaped ditches that are so unique to Northwest Ohio were seemingly custom-made to deliver this key ingredient of toxic algae to Lake Erie.

Fertilizer is loaded with phosphorus, but the element phosphorus, in its basic form, is pretty harmless. Like cyanobacteria, it serves an essential purpose to life on Earth. For instance, plenty of plants thrive on phosphorus; it helps countless species grow, which is why it is found in fertilizer. However, too much phosphorus leads to toxic algae, and Lake Erie seems to be getting more than its share. A *Guardian* report noted that it "received the most phosphorus of any of the Great Lakes—44% of the total for all of the lakes."

This presents the question: Why don't we *fix* the corn or the way it's farmed? It turns out that demanding farmers or scientists simply fix the problem is some seriously magical thinking. "I think sometimes what gets lost is the complexity of the system a farmer is dealing with," one expert told the CBC.

While it may seem like the easy answer would be to curb fertilizer, in 2014 NPR cited a report that fertilizer usage had already been in decline over the previous decade. Farmers are not ignorant of the repercussions here and seem to be making an effort, one of many reasons likely being environmental. So, in theory, this decline in fertilizer should mean that the algae problem would be decreasing, not multiplying. Yet there was that more than 218 percent increase in phosphorus. What gives?

"The amount of phosphorous that is lost per year is directly related to the amount of precipitation we get," NPR said. "And as we have had more extreme events and more precipitation events in the past years, we have had more runoff and more algae bloom."

In essence, less fertilizer is being applied, which is great. However, larger rates of precipitation because of climate change mean that a higher percentage of that fertilizer is getting into the lake. In 2014, the US Agriculture Department's Steve Davis noted, "We're not losing excessive amounts per acre, compared to even other areas in the country. But we have so many acres draining into one spot." The increase in precipitation and warmer lake temperatures are both attributed to global warming. And when they collide, we get harmful algae blooms.

"Imagine you're at an all-you-can-eat buffet, and you gorge yourself," says Jennifer Caddick, the director of the Alliance for Great Lakes. "That's what's happening with this algae."

The suspects for this toxic algae case are quickly growing to Agatha Christie levels of complexity. For those keeping score at home:

First, it was farmers.

Next, it was corn.

Then phosphorus.

Now, it's global warming.

In reality, it's not any single one of these but a combination of all the suspects at once. Northwest Ohio was once a million-acre uninhabited wetland region that gently filtered this water and slowly drained it into Lake Erie. Now it's a million-acre Molotov cocktail of phosphorus rapidly flushing into that one vulnerable destination. Essentially, now that the Great Black Swamp is no more, the area is the worst place in the world for all this runoff.

When you begin to look at the picture as a whole, the sensible conclusion seems to be: "Let's just regulate them. Isn't that the government's job?"

Yes and no.

"When we bring this subject up for conversation with the regulators, everyone sort of walks out of the room," Donald Moline, then the Toledo commissioner of public utilities, told *The New York Times* shortly after the 2014 outbreak. It doesn't take a lot of poking and prodding to see that there is really no benefit for politicians to crack down on the causes of toxic algae. If they did, they'd disrupt agricultural industries that are vital to the economy, which would also result in food prices skyrocketing—which would likely result in political chaos. But, just for argument's sake, let's say the government stepped in and really solved this problem, and toxic algae vanished. More than likely, voters wouldn't give credit to their representatives in Congress. So, really, what's the government's motivation?

Even scarier for Toledoans who enjoy drinking uncontaminated water, *The Washington Post* noted, is that "there are no national standards for algal cyanotoxin in drinking water. U.S. utilities don't need to test for it. How widespread the toxin is in drinking water is a mystery."

In a strange way, when you consider the stunning rise of toxic algae worldwide, this unheralded portion of Ohio is showing the entire planet the causes and effects of toxic algae in one tidy microcosm.

Though Toledo just survived an ecological catastrophe in that microcosm, that familiar amnesiac thinking quickly kicked into gear back in 2014. While the town was still recovering from this terrifying brush with disaster, tough Toledoans shrugged, smiled, and did the unthinkable. They went back to normal.

7
THE CARIBBEAN SEA OF THE MIDWEST

I mean, really, it was fine," says the first person I meet who actually witnessed the 2014 algae crisis. She wears a blue embroidered polo shirt and sits behind the front desk of the National Museum of the Great Lakes. She was in middle school in 2014. "I remember it being, like, everyone was freaking out and hoarding bottled water."

The museum sits on the Maumee River, nestled among the Mondelez plant and the PBF refinery I passed earlier. The building is sleekly modern and features several nice exhibits on boating and weather-related historical moments across all five Great Lakes. I ask if the museum has any information about the 2014 algae bloom, but it doesn't. I wander the museum, learning about the evolution of maritime technology on the lakes and of shipwrecks on the lakes, famous locales along their shores, endlessly charmed by these sea stories. Even though I grew up an hour from these waters, I spent almost no time on them or even thinking about them. So there's something exotic about it all for a boy who grew up surrounded by a sea of corn.

After buying a book in the gift shop, I press the clerk more about 2014.

"I wasn't too shocked about it," she says.

"Why?"

"I mean, Maumee Bay, that beach has been opened and closed our entire lives. So, I mean, it sounds bad, but I was kind of like 'Okay. What else is new?' Like, that's why we never went swimming in Maumee Bay."

I tell the clerk that I'm surprised, because all the newspapers made the toxic algae sound pretty hellish at the time. Weren't you scared or angry? She shrugs and pinches her eyes in a way that suggests I'm a wimp.

Across town, at a small public boat launch right on Lake Erie's shore, three retirees rest in camping chairs shaded by a huge tree. These friendly folks chitchat with me about the heat and, eventually, toxic algae.

"It was kind of blown out of proportion," says Sandy. She's in a sleeveless yellow blouse and never touches the pack of Marlboros beside her. "There were many factories around here that dumped into the water. That made it worse. Most of the factories are gone now."

That same nautical smell as the beach rolls in. I notice behind them, across the bay, are the same oil refinery stacks I saw earlier. Even though the industrial components of the town are diminished, it's like you can't escape them.

She compares pre-2014 Lake Erie to a cruise she took to the Caribbean back in the 1970s, specifically how they'd just dump the boat's trash and toilet waste directly into the ocean. "Now we've got all these megafarms that should be outlawed instead of just dumping all the manure and everything. I have no use for a megafarm. I think it's terrible."

Another woman, Sophia, practically gags, saying that the 2014 water was "yucky." Sandy agrees and tells a story of piloting her small fishing boat through the algae during the water scare.

"Wow," I say, confused. I assumed every Toledoan was holed up at home, praying to survive this disaster. It never occurred to me that some folks were out on the lake like it was any normal Saturday in August. All my articles and YouTube clips don't mention people partaking in water sports. "Was it scary, going through the lake in your boat?"

I step gingerly to the side, trying to find a patch of shade to stand in.

"No, it wasn't scary," says Sandy. "I mean, we knew what it was." She pauses and sneers, as if maybe she is still holding a grudge: "But it sure made a mess out of the bottom of the boat."

Next, I go across town and take shelter inside a mercifully air-conditioned gift shop on Lake Erie's shore. Stepping inside feels like being pleasantly dunked in cool water. "It looked like pea soup when you were going through with your boat and it's throwing the water up," says a manager in a teal polo shirt and khaki shorts. Billy Joel plays softly through the overhead speakers. He checks a clipboard, eager to return to stocking the shelves with Lake Erie–branded shot glasses and hats. "You just hate it because it ruins boating."

I can't think of another question. My brain has stalled. These recollections are chilling and yet the most Northwest Ohio thing I have ever heard.

He fills the silence: "It's ridiculous because you don't want to go in there. You don't want to Jet Ski because people were getting it in their mouth. You don't want your dogs to go out swimming."

I slink off back to the boiling hot Hyundai, still plucking mayflies off my shirt. All around town I ask several more strangers, "Were you scared? I'd have been really scared." Toledoans of different stripes tell me: No, it wasn't that bad being waterless for three days. (Usually accompanied by that now-familiar squint or tone of voice implying that I'm being dramatic.) "Yeah," everyone says in one way or another, "we kind of expected something like this to happen, what with the way our city is run. Yeah, it'll probably happen again. No biggie."

I'm surprised, but also not surprised. In my experience, Northwest Ohio greets pretty much any problem, from a leaky roof to a loved one's terminal illness, with this "No big deal. Don't be dramatic" state of mind.

I have been accused of being dramatic before. In high school, as a sensitive, creative weirdo desperately trying to fit in, I would blurt out things that seemed to always win me similar looks as these Toledoans. When I get that look, it's like a sweaty, blinding spotlight has hit me. I panic, get fidgety, and say something self-deprecating, praying the other person will let me slide. I frequently found myself mixed up in toxic relationships like that, where people I thought were my best friends would squint and say hurtful things to let me know I was not being normal. It's like I'm being punished for wrecking that no-big-deal ambivalence.

As I grew from a sensitive, creative, weird child into a sensitive, creative, weird adult, I was still drawn into toxic relationships where those closest to me made me feel small and misguided and stupid. It gets to the point where it often feels like I'm only comfortable when I'm low status, lying deep in the mud, nearly invisible. While I am up in Toledo, I don't realize that my sixteen-year marriage to my college sweetheart is falling apart for similar reasons. A few months after getting back from Ohio, I have never been more in love with my wife. Out of the blue one evening, she tells me she doesn't think she loves me anymore but is not sure—she might also want to stay together too.

I dealt with this confusing, heartbreaking news in the same way any sensitive weirdo would: I stood up for myself and walked away from this troubled situation!

I'm kidding.

I went into low-status mode, willingly crawling through the mud. I also started crying. Crying so much that my eyes ached for hours afterward. Tearing up multiple times a day for the next several months for the slightest reason. Whenever I started bawling in front of my wife or begging her to give me an answer so I could stop hurting, I often got a similar response as in Toledo. If she responded at all, I would end up feeling like I was being dramatic. This just made me more frantic to fix it, to take all the blame and—at all costs—keep this unhealthy relationship going in order to keep my life normal.

Back in Toledo, the sense that I'm being dramatic makes me second-guess myself, as always. Folks continue to surprise me with their no-big-whoop tales of the toxic algae crisis. A record store clerk remembers his high school government teacher claiming toxic algae was a conspiracy by, of course, the government. Another woman complains about getting diarrhea after drinking a friend's well water instead of her poisonous tap water. A guy being dragged along by several dogs at a park tells me he took a shower when the government said not to and nothing bad happened.

The entire day I only found one person who admitted to being even slightly rattled. "I was nervous, yeah," says the manager of Tony Packo's as I dig into my chicken paprikash and breathe a sigh of relief that maybe I'm not the only sensitive weirdo in town.

I'm actually sitting beneath a huge photo of the cast of *M*A*S*H** in costume at the craft services table of their soundstage, wolfing down chili dogs, which were flown from Toledo to Hollywood sometime in the 1970s. Tony Packo's, also nestled in that industrial corridor of oil refineries and flour mills, has inexplicably become a destination for famous visitors of a certain era—the walls are lined with hundreds of autographed hot dog buns by everyone from Burt Reynolds to Carrot Top to Danny Kaye. I do not see John Denver's signature, though. The whole place smells delightfully like paprika and sausage. Tiffany chandeliers hang from the ceiling.

I ask the manager if he was scared.

He half shrugs and says it was not too bad. "My main thing was they said it was okay to wash your laundry in it, but I was like, 'I don't know, man.'"

He waits a beat, the same way Johnny Carson did when Denver botched his softball joke about Toledo in 1973. I guess the manager wants me to share in his laundry-related suffering, and I emphatically agree out of sheer politeness and a hatred of making anyone feel uncomfortable. I side with him that, yes, not doing laundry for nearly half a week sounds like hell, but secretly wonder, *What is going on around here?* I was under the impression the algae crisis was the worst thing that ever happened. Instead, it's as if nothing happened. I love

Northwest Ohio, but sometimes it feels like I'm speaking a different language than everyone from my home.

Businessmen storm into the dining room, plates stacked with hot dogs and pierogies, all with a side of paprika ranch dressing, slurping Pepsi from beveled red plastic glasses, loudly discussing quarterly figures. There's an urge to ask for their 2014 experiences, but I know the answer.

Maybe the Toledo algae crisis wasn't such a big deal?

Maybe I am being dramatic?

I head over to the Tony Packo's gift shop and buy my ten-year-old son a pen shaped like a pickle. Usually, a green gherkin pen would make me laugh, but not today. I'm stewing in all these heartbreaking reminders of my outsiderness. It's how I felt when I was being bullied as a teenager, and how I feel today, and how I will soon feel going through my inevitable divorce. It's like the rest of the world is normal and I am not. Like there's something wrong with the way I filter everything.

How did Toledo go from near-death experience for four hundred thousand people to such ambivalence? How did I become someone so desperately eager to please that I am living the same life that I'm criticizing in so many others?

PART III

The temptation to glorify a small town is great when you don't live in one. And so, for that matter, is the temptation to satirize it if you do.... Neither approach will get you very close to the truth.

—David Dempsey

8
VERNAL POOLS

I should have brought a machete," Melanie says over her shoulder, half-joking and half-serious as we work our way through the chaotic, leafy brush.

"I can't imagine why," I say, catching a branch swinging back that nearly gives me a concussion as we hunt for the remains of the Great Black Swamp.

The weather report now says *today* is actually the hottest non-summer day in Northwest Ohio history—almost triple digits, unthinkable heat for June. It's just after breakfast, and the thick, humid air feels like punishment despite the strong wind—a powerful gale that forces us to shout just to hear each other. Sweat stings my eyes as we slowly navigate the overgrown grass. Melanie shoves through dense walls of emerald-colored ferns, trillium, and stinging nettle, searching for our trailhead without much success. The sun is so strong that even beneath a faded red ball cap her transition lenses have turned the color of smoke. I am jealous of her waterproof rubber galoshes, decorated in a pale red octopus pattern. Each foot makes a sucking noise when it pulls from the black mud.

Our search has barely even started and already my tennis shoes are soaking wet. I regret not packing better.

Boots? Absolutely.

Some huge, vine-slashing machete? Yes.

Bug spray? For sure. A gallon of bug spray, the atomic kind absolutely swimming with DEET.

We are walking along the outskirts of Bell Woods, an eighty-acre nature preserve about twenty miles south of Lake Erie. The forest is boxed in on all sides by wheat fields stretching into the horizon. You wouldn't know it by looking around today at the vast, agriculturally abundant Northwest Ohio landscape, but this place was once so prehistorically wild and deadly that it took nearly a century of struggle to finally bend this land to Manifest Destiny's will. The process was a nightmarish undertaking, filled with suffering, broken hearts, death, and both our best and worst American impulses. Today, outside of small preserves like this, it seems like this landscape was simply born a million acres of perfectly level fields of corn, soybeans, and wheat. Growing up, that's what I always thought. Which is why I need someone like Melanie to teach me.

Melanie Coulter is an expert on forgotten places like Bell Woods. She is the conservation manager for Black Swamp Conservancy, a small land trust that has tasked itself with the difficult job of trying to save Lake Erie and the surrounding area one plot of land at a time. Melanie began working with the organization in 2017 and has more than twenty years of experience in habitat restoration. There are few people who understand this ecosystem better. Even if she can't completely remember where the entrance to the woods is hidden.

After a few minutes, we finally bushwhack deep enough to find the crude trail, and instantly the entire forest opens up and the rushing wind goes silent. This feels like stepping into an entirely different, secret world. Under the tree canopy it's all peaceful birdsong and soft rustling leaves. It smells like fresh mulch. Our feet sink into an endless stretch of dark mud speckled with little green plumes of some tiny plant I can't name that looks like clover on steroids. This forest is complex and beautiful in a way that makes me feel a little bit bouncy, despite my curdling feet. The trees are so dense I can't stick out a hand without touching a trunk.

"What are all these?" I say, taking a shot. "Like, oak trees?"

"That is a shagbark hickory." She points quickly. "Sycamores. Beeches. There's a lot of old big trees, but then also a lot of young trees underneath." As we continue, Melanie refers to the skinny young ones as *babies*, the mature ones as *old guys*, and the entire ecosystem as a *community*. "And so, it creates a pretty dark forest. Not a lot of light's getting down to the understory here."

That darkness makes the woods feel easily ten degrees cooler than when we were out in the sun. Everything is coated in shadow, except for thin spotlights racing down through the leaves. This place was famous for its distinct lack of daylight. Supposedly, back in the bad old days, the canopy was so thick you couldn't tell day from night, which is one theory as to how this region earned the name the Great Black Swamp.

"Is this about how dark it was back then?" I say.

"I don't know. Dark is a hard thing to quantify. I would say that it was as dark as just after sunset. But not like pitch dark. You could still see your hand in front of you."

I can easily see my hand. While it's a massive improvement over the Trautman Nature Center, I sink a little deeper into the mud, wishing this place was more nightmarish.

To fully understand 2014's algae crisis, we need to find a swamp that looks nothing like what people think of when they picture this overlooked corner of the state. According to experts, that God-awful swamp that early Northwest Ohioans spent decades trying to destroy could have prevented Lake Erie's poisoning. And I want to see that for myself. The Northwest Ohio I want is the one circa 1820, the one that sounds like a stoned teenager describing a heavy metal album cover. The Great Black Swamp was once regarded as one of the most dangerous places in America. It was huge—roughly the size of Connecticut—and not only dark but also filled with treacherous mud six feet deep across its entire breadth. It was also full of man-eating creatures and swarms of malaria-infected mosquitos. By some accounts, it was the last uninhabited stretch of land east of the Mississippi River, even later than the Everglades.

As we walk deeper into the woods, Melanie points out other tree species, including an oak, which feels like a victory and makes me think maybe I'm not a total idiot. Maybe I do belong out here? Just a little? Though to be honest, I still kind of feel like a fraud, not even wise enough to pack something other than my best sneakers. But I'm learning quickly, despite the fact that I am not an environmentalist or a scientist and the last time I took a biology course was freshman year of college, twenty-five years ago, for which I scored a C+.

Emboldened by the oak tree find, I throw out one of the few other ecology words I have picked up recently, asking if these are *old growth*.

"No, not old growth," she says. There is apparently no such thing as old growth around here anymore. The Great Black Swamp was drained and logged into obliteration at the start of the twentieth century. But most people who grew up here were barely even taught that history, myself included. But, Melanie assures me, these trees are still extremely old, among the oldest we know of, "except for maybe Goll Woods."

I make a mental note of that name, Goll Woods, as a white-tailed deer jumps off. The underbrush is so thick that the deer's shiny brown hide is completely invisible after a few graceful, silent leaps. Seeing one is not uncommon, of course, though supposedly herds of deer once ran through this area in packs so large it took minutes for them to pass, almost like a bison stampede. That lone deer gives me hope that maybe a scrap of the Great Black Swamp still exists somewhere.

"Look out, it's pretty squishy here," she says.

I step carefully across a gooey black mix of soil, decayed forest, and two inches of recent rainfall. No matter what path I take, I'm always up to my shoe tops in mud. Melanie says we're lucky: in March it went above her calf. Still, that's nothing compared to what was once here.

She recommends avoiding those pockets of standing dark water known as vernal pools because those go way deeper than they look. We take a minute to admire one, and she explains that a vernal pool forms when water fills the huge cavity left behind after a dead tree falls over. The water's surface shimmers with what little light sneaks through. Dragonflies circle, hunting for a meal. She tells me places like Bell Woods are full of overlooked little things that are crucial to an ecosystem's livelihood. Everything's connected, even when it doesn't appear that way.

She points toward rare salamanders skittering nearby and explains that all those endless green sprouts, the ones I thought were clover on steroids, are wild ginger, one of the few native plants still found around Northwest Ohio.

As we wander, Melanie says she and her husband are amateur beer brewers. She enthusiastically tells me about their recent obsession with adding surprising local ingredients, like sumac, to their ales. As we continue through this swampy, but not Black Swamp-y, woods she explains the complex, vibrant interconnectedness of life in a Northwest Ohio wetland with that same enthusiasm. But my mind drifts. There's a dark, vernal pool in my brain that I can't seem to shake.

I don't feel connected to this land the way I thought I would upon returning. The ex-Catholic in me had a hunch that suffering would be the doorway to enlightenment, which I think is a big reason why I want to know what this place was like two hundred years ago, back when it had a national reputation for mud that swallowed horses alive, gangs of bloodthirsty wolves, and a malaria rate so deadly that grim poems were written about it. Maybe if I suffer enough, I'll reconnect?

››››››

Growing up, I felt deeply connected to my home. Connected, despite (or maybe because of) being alone quite a lot. The Wensink homestead was three miles outside of Deshler on Road F, with no other houses for at least a mile in every direction. So, whenever I was playing outside, or up in a tree, or building a fort, I was alone. I ran around with imaginary friends because I didn't have any real ones. And I couldn't have been happier.

Dad worked at the Ball factory in Findlay, the aluminum soda can division of the famous Ball mason jar makers. He was a thin, dark-haired Air Force vet who loved NASCAR so much that in the days before every race was on national television he'd record it on AM radio and listen to the cassette later. He volunteered as an EMT and as my T-ball coach and was a member of several bowling leagues. There was never a single song that he didn't know the name of the artist for and most of the words to.

Mom was a homemaker until she started working at the town library while I was in elementary school. In the 1980s, she sheared her long hair for a tight, modern perm. She was a trim brunette with glasses the size of drink coasters, and she was the most sarcastic person I knew. She would patiently explain the gag in each day's *Far Side* comic in the *Toledo Blade*. She picked up acrylic painting and created peaceful, rustic scenes of covered bridges, Mail Pouch barns, and lonely fenceposts. It was the only art I was exposed to until visiting the Musée d'Orsay on a study abroad trip to France during college.

My sister, Jenny, was five years older and always seemed to be at school. Either going to it or sticking around after school playing volleyball, or basketball, or softball. She never missed an episode of *L.A. Law* and was focused on becoming a lawyer someday. She and her girlfriends listened to pop music obsessively, and they let me tag along with them for my first concert: Milli Vanilli at the Toledo Sports Arena.

In the late summer, corn stretched so high that our entire property was often boxed in by rustling green stalks, making the air smell like raw soil and corn husk. When a breeze blew, the ears rubbed together so that the world sounded like a big seashell. In the winter, a good snowfall filled up the ditches and erased the single-lane road beside our house; the ripping prairie wind could fill our doorway with a small snowdrift overnight.

Deshler was rural, but because my house was surrounded by endless farm fields, we were even more isolated, which meant that in school I was considered a "country kid." A sort of factual, sort of derogatory term. Since there were no nearby children to play with in this pre–cable TV, pre-Nintendo, rotary phone era, I had no choice but to be deeply rooted to our little square acre of land. My main preoccupation was leading that posse of imaginary friends through the yard and up craggy, low-slung apple trees. Not to boast, but this ragtag crew once included Kenny Rogers after I watched the TV movie *The Gambler* one night. That was not unusual. When not immersing myself in imaginary play, I sat open-jawed in front of whatever television station could be coaxed from a skeletal antenna atop our roof. Unless it was Saturday morning cartoons on the major networks, the best station was PBS. On the days when the weather was clear enough that the Toledo and Bowling Green affiliates stretched their signals to Deshler, I soaked up anything that fizzled through public broadcasting's schedule. From *Sesame Street* and *3-2-1 Contact* to *This Old House* and *Sewing with Nancy*—I loved them all equally. At this time, I was a chubber. Thick in the cheeks and thick in the thighs. Most mornings my thick little rump was glued to the carpet, holding my stuffed brown bear, Jehoshaphat.

My parents were loving and permissive, and home was a stable place. They weren't big on yelling or punishing me, even though I probably deserved both. This peaceful, isolated country life allowed me the freedom to develop at my own pace and live in my own weirdness since there were no neighbor kids to compare myself to. I didn't know what was or was not normal.

When I was about three, Mom found me rummaging around our sunflower-yellow refrigerator at eight o'clock in the morning. "What are you doing, Pat?" she said, peering over the door at my little towheaded, freckled face. "Just getting a beer and watching *Mr. Rogers*!" I replied, as if it were something I did every morning at this time.

Once, my sister was shooting foul shots by the garage and caught me standing on a picnic table, strumming a softball bat like a guitar as thousands of fans cheered on my imaginary band. Kenny Rogers and I had started a supergroup and were currently singing a duet of the hardest-rocking song I knew at the time, "Blue Suede Shoes." She did her job as cooler older sibling and told me I was being weird. It was the first time I felt the pangs of shame for acting the way I acted. But instead of lashing out or crying, I tried being normal.

Even though I was over an hour from Lake Erie, I did play near water. Water, for me, meant exploring those deep, V-shaped drainage ditches that were big enough to swallow a car. When it wasn't raining, the water level would drop to a trickle, and you could find cattails and collect the patches of little gelatinous frog eggs in a bucket or explore the massive concrete culvert tunnels that ran beneath the roads. Not exactly Tom Sawyer on the Mississippi, but it was my version of normal. And stable. And happy. I knew every tree and rock and aspect of my landscape.

I've been aching to reconnect like that lately. Soon, this return to Northwest Ohio will become more than a research trip; this will become the only place my life feels like it has any control or stability.

Shortly after I return, my wife will move out of our house and will keep my heart suspended on the surface between hope and agony, love and pain, divorce and marriage for longer than I am capable of withstanding. Up until this point, I had never been more in love with her, and this proves to be a disaster I am unprepared for. In order to keep above water, I start employing a skill that is baked into my Northwest Ohio DNA. I look on the bright side, telling myself this marital disruption is normal and that it'll pass. I sometimes chastise myself for overreacting and being dramatic.

I was hoping this return home would root me in reality, maybe give me some firm ground to stand on, but it's having the opposite effect. It's starting to seem like I can't connect with anyone, anything, or any place.

I slap at my cheek, and my arm, and my ear because a platoon of mosquitoes has decided that today is my funeral. I am continually ducking from what sounds like a pair of barbershop clippers in my ear. I forgot to apply bug spray, and the mosquitos are taunting me before they suck my blood. My lower lip and arms throb from bites. I kill one on my elbow and it leaves a bright red stain big enough to require a chalk outline.

"Settlers used to cover themselves in bear grease to avoid being stung," Melanie says. Back then, malaria rates were brutal, and swarms of mosquitoes were so thick that some mistook them for clouds of smoke.

I tell her I'd pay a thousand bucks for a can of grizzly lard right now. We continue on, and she explains that natural wetlands like this, even though they are not *exactly* like what the Great Black Swamp used to be, are incredibly important. So important that some say they are one of the few things keeping another 2014 algae crisis from happening. More intriguing, places like Bell Woods could be the cure to this area's environmental concerns.

"Did you," Melanie asks, "spend a lot of time in the woods growing up around here?"

I pause a minute and feel my socks go as damp as dishrags. My instinct is to say, "Yes!" because I was constantly playing outside. I was always in a tree, or building a fort, or running around with imaginary friends. But that's not the woods, and saying yes would be a lie. It's become pretty clear that I've been pretty oblivious about things I thought were true.

"No, almost none," I say. "Where I grew up, I think that's pretty typical. People just don't think about the land. I had hardly any exposure to nature as a kid, which you wouldn't think growing up in the country."

Melanie suggests we drive three counties over to a microscopic town called Evansport, where there is a site the Black Swamp Conservancy is working on. It's not a remnant of the Great Black Swamp like I'm hunting for but something far more unique. And far more relevant to the 2014 algae crisis.

I tell her that sounds great. But that I have to stop at a library first.

9
THE DARK HALF

Bowling Green is the unofficial capital of the Great Black Swamp region.

Yes, Toledo's population is over thirteen times larger, but Toledo is really on the fringe of the swamp. Swamp-adjacent? The swamp-burbs, let's say. Bowling Green is the closest thing to a city within its murky borders, even though calling it a city is pushing the limits of the word. College town is a better description. This afternoon, Bowling Green State University's campus is empty because it's summer, and the Jerome Library is so dead the student worker at the front desk looks a little surprised to see another living soul.

I plan to spend my day high up on the fifth floor where the archives are housed, digging through Black Swamp history. The archive room is long, skinny, and so silent the filament can be heard bouncing around the overhead lights. This wing of the library looks like it hasn't been remodeled since Richard Nixon guest-starred on *Laugh-In*.

"Do you get a lot of people looking for this kind of stuff?" I ask Sarah, the kind, softspoken librarian wearing a black COVID mask.

"No," she says. "Hardly ever. Most people just want photos for genealogy."

"Nobody seems to think about this stuff much, huh?"

She doesn't reply and quietly disappears into a back room. Sarah returns with a squeaky metal cart stacked with everything I requested: old news clippings, books, file folders of handwritten letters, a ship's log for the *John G. Deshler*, a board game called "The Great Black Swamp," and a few VHS tapes, including one labeled *The Story of the Great Black Swamp*.

I can't resist the board game and pop it open first.

The glossy gameboard is most likely homemade, though mounted on professional-looking cardstock. Searches online for its manufacturer, the Junior Achievement Company of Defiance, Ohio, turn up nothing, save for a dead entry in Boardgamegeek.com. The game is printed with meandering red and green and yellow spaces, which looks similar to LIFE but themed like a hand-drawn version of *Oregon Trail*. The goal, as best I can tell since the instructions are partially missing, is to get a treaty with the British and Native Americans signed and returned to Fort Defiance without dying. I'm happily amused by penalty squares like "Musketoes Aplenty, GO BACK 2 SPACES," even though it's hitting pretty close to home, since I still have several red welts from Bell Woods. But knowing how these treaties turned out for the Native tribes leaves me feeling depressed and gross for being so amused in the first place. I box it up and try to keep things happy and normal and productive.

Next, I'm drawn to *The Story of the Great Black Swamp*.

Much like the board game, this title has little to no online footprint. I quickly move to the cramped audio/visual room and shove this tape into a VCR. It weirdly reminds me of the thrill of renting a movie as a kid and that moment of anticipation before a film chugs to life. I have no idea what it could be: a historic reenactment? A cartoon on par with *Schoolhouse Rock!* productions? A tape of some local stage play I have never heard of? Regardless, I'm weirdly nervous and excited that something like *The Story of the Great Black Swamp* exists at all. Movies aren't made about Northwest Ohio.

When the film begins it feels about as exhilarating as a Hollywood premiere. Even though I am currently struggling for a connection, I have always loved this place. I developed such a deep affection for Ohio that my years on the West Coast were often spent defending this state's greatness. Anyone scoffing at Ohio would hear me go into long stories about how Play-Doh was invented here! The Etch A Sketch was imported from France and manufactured here! We gave the world Devo, the barcode, Rob Lowe, the vacuum cleaner, the stepladder, Halle Berry, Smucker's Jam, Toni Morrison, Quaker Oats, and Trent Reznor! That means the lead singer of Nine Inch Nails probably once bought Quaker Oats in his hometown of Cleveland, and someone at the grocery store scanned its barcode. Wrap your mind around that!

Coworkers and friends in Arizona, Oregon, Kentucky, and Tennessee never seemed all that impressed.

One story I never told them was about Northwest Ohio's terrifying history. Primarily because I didn't know it until recently. Maybe Mr. Gar covered some Black Swamp stories in Ohio History class, but they didn't stick. Probably because history and regional pride were not a part of daily life in Northwest Ohio. Why didn't they show *The Story of the Great Black Swamp* in the school auditorium? Why wasn't it screened in the city park every summer? Why hadn't I at least seen it on PBS while watching such an absurd amount of PBS as a boy?

The film turns out to be an hourlong 1982 documentary and I am instantly obsessed. This movie is brilliant because it doesn't just illustrate the swamp's history; it also wants to share darker secrets about my home. But, hush, its filmmakers don't just come out and dish the dirt. That's not how we do things in Northwest Ohio. Like the swamp's history itself, there are a lot of things hidden by a desire to keep everything normal on the surface.

Our host is a calm, white-haired man named Glenn Colerider who delivers each line in a folksy voice fit for a Smucker's commercial. Every syllable from Glenn's thin lips is a warm hug. He wants to be your grandpa for the next hour. Let him.

"If you've ever traveled through Northwest Ohio," he says, "you've probably been struck by how flat the land is here." My toes ball up in excitement. I feel so seen.

He's right. A five-story building like the Jerome Library is a skyscraper in the land of the Great Black Swamp. Out the AV room's window I can see all the way to the horizon line, and save for a few tufts of trees and a farmhouse, it's nothing but green and golden acreage in every direction. *Great Black Swamp*'s cold open finds Glenn standing knee-deep in some swaying farm field like that, with the endless expanse of Ohio behind him. Northwest Ohio's fields are unmatched. The only places I've seen that rival its empty flatness in America are Death Valley, the Mississippi Delta, and West Texas—but those usually have *some* elevation change, a few gently rolling hills at the least. Not here. It's so flat here that from my childhood backyard I could spot several towns' Fourth of July fireworks simply by staring across the landscape, even though they were usually over a dozen miles away.

The Story of the Great Black Swamp is a production of the university's film program. The documentary was shot on what appears to be some bargain bin film stock full of grit and grain and poor lighting, which I find to be quite charming in a DIY, let's-put-on-a-show way. Glenn's wardrobe consists of a blue and yellow checkered shirt and a pair of double-knit trousers that look as if they were purchased at Kmart. He is skinny as a cornstalk, so when the wind rolls off the fields it makes the shirt flap like it's about a size too big.

His *aw-shucks* narration introduces us to the agricultural bounty of the land, but he also emphasizes that this place was once an "abysmal, human-forsaken swamp." According to Glenn, some of the biblical plague–worthy things about my homeland included homicidal amounts of mosquitoes, and wolves, and snakes, and wildcats, and gnats, and horseflies, and moccasins, and water rats, and vines, and mosquitoes, and bears, and mud, and downed trees, and SO MANY MOSQUITOES.

Visions of bear grease dance through my head as Glenn's soft voice, full of wisdom and awe, calls the settling of this hellscape a heroic conquest. "The people here treated the Great Black Swamp as though it were the enemy and they annihilated it, and the swamp, in turn, took a part of the soul of everyone who touched it."

Wait, what?

Glenn Colerider, who died in 2012 at age eighty-five, was a beloved community theater actor around Cleveland, and he also landed a small role in the George Romero movie *The Dark Half*, based on Stephen King's novel. His character in that movie, Homer Gamache, is also a doddering, likeable grandpa type, but a grandpa-type photographer with a passion for shooting pictures of teddy bears lying in coffins. "I want to make them into a book," the Gamache character says. "The final, perfect comment on the American way of...*death*." About five minutes later, Homer gets yanked out of a pickup truck window and murdered with his own wooden leg by Timothy Hutton. Up on the fifth floor, it becomes instantly clear how Glenn landed that horror flick role, because with this soul-stealing line he is giving off a similar vibe. Intense darkness masked by a veil of boring normalcy. A perfect fit for Northwest Ohio.

And that's not even mentioning *The Story of the Great Black Swamp*'s soundtrack. For a film already leaning pretty hard on the greatness of the area's farmland, you'd maybe expect a quaint banjo and harmonica duet for the opening credit sequence. But when the introduction ends, Glenn's sunbeaten face stares down the barrel of the camera as an eerie, brooding synthesizer creeps in—a tone piece right out of *The Terminator* or *Halloween*. Today, it sounds vintage or even corny, but four decades ago it was probably an homage to the dangerous, futuristic compositions of John Carpenter and Tangerine Dream. The scuzzy synth intro continues for thirty seconds like it is soundtracking an axe murder—but instead of gore, the screen cycles between production credits and shots of tractors tearing up the land. Then, just as the title card appears, the camera unexpectedly shifts to a first-person POV from inside a hole filling with dirt.

It's only the three-minute mark, and the Great Black Swamp is already taking our soul and burying us alive.

10

HERE IS THE PLACE GOD FORGOT

Glenn's not wrong. The Great Black Swamp has, indeed, been home to soullessness, crime, and even treason. Nobody embodies this darkness more clearly than Simon Girty, one of the most notorious villains of eighteenth-century America. Girty, it turns out, was often mentioned in the same vindictive breath as Benedict Arnold back then. A man so evil that parents across the young nation would warn their children to be good or "Simon Girty will come get you."

Simon Girty was born in 1741 in Pennsylvania, where he was taken captive by the Seneca tribe as a teenager. He then moved to Ohio, where he assimilated and became a member of the tribe, eventually fighting for the Native Americans and British during the Revolutionary War. Girty earned his villain status thanks to reports that he helped torture American prisoners. He took particular glee and vindictiveness in the act, if accounts are to be believed. While Girty was seen as treasonous at the time, historians now view him with a little more complexity, as someone doing these awful deeds to defend Native people's rights to their land. A villain and a hero.

One oil painting of Girty reflects this complicated life, presenting him as if he were Johnny Depp's *Pirates of the Caribbean* stunt double. Broad-shouldered and strong-jawed, Girty wears a jaunty red bandana wrapped around his head, and several Native American pouches and woven belts hang across his wide chest. Most notably, he sports two fat hoop earrings and a septum ring. But he also wears a more European-looking coat and has a bayonet rifle over his shoulder. If this is even a fraction of how the actual man appeared, he must have seemed like an alien.

Girty would frequently use the Great Black Swamp as cover, hiding from the law on a small island on the Maumee River just upstream from Napoleon, Ohio, not far from where I grew up, sometimes for long stretches at a time. Today, Girty's Island is just a clump of trees in the middle of the water. There used to be a historical marker, but it seems to have been stolen. In other parts of the country, this story would be brought into the light for examination, even celebration, like how Benedict Arnold has his own historic walking trail in Connecticut and the annual Benedict Arnold's Raid reenactment in Richmond, Virginia. Instead, Girty died in 1818 and apparently faded from memory for all but the most historically minded in the region.

On that same note, it's equally surprising there isn't an attraction dedicated to Harry Pierpont in Northwest Ohio. While Girty is easily our most notable bad guy, Pierpont, from Leipsic, a town fifteen minutes from Deshler, should be known as our most notorious criminal. He was an infamous 1930s bank robber, but nowhere nearly as well-known as his boss, John Dillinger.

Pierpont and Dillinger became friends in jail, and in 1933, after both escaped prison, they robbed between ten and twenty banks in

Northwest Ohio, using Pierpont's Leipsic farm as a hideout. Both were captured, and Pierpont was put to death in 1934 for the murder of a sheriff's deputy during one robbery. Dillinger was famously shot to death by the FBI later that year. Rumors began swirling immediately that their loot was still buried somewhere near that Leipsic farmhouse. "The farmland of northwestern Ohio hardly seems fertile ground for buried treasure," the *Chicago Tribune* wrote in 1988. "But one farm near here has been the target of treasure hunters for more than 53 years."

In other parts of America, this could have been the start of a cottage tourism industry akin to the bullet-riddled Bonnie and Clyde Death Car in Primm, Nevada, or the possibility of finding a real-life *Goonies* treasure of lost gold doubloons on the Oregon coast. But this is Ohio, the Heart of It All, the capital of not drawing attention to oneself. "People, adventurist types, came from all over the place—New York, Pennsylvania—and searched for the money," one former neighbor told the *Tribune*. "I don't know if there's anything there. Might be, but I doubt it."

Echoing that sentiment, the owner of the Pierponts' land made about the most Northwest Ohio statement imaginable: "If they buried it, I'll bet someone came back and got it. I've never spent a minute looking for it."

In 1997, even I caught the soulless criminal bug still floating around the former Black Swamp. I was arrested one spring evening while standing in the parking lot of Deshler's only pizza restaurant, Pisanello's. It was a few hours after the shop had closed, and several cooler teens were having an impromptu party there. Deshler was often so sleepy in the 1990s that it wasn't unheard of for carloads of kids to congregate in a parking lot and drink beer, smoke cigarettes, and blast country or heavy metal music from car stereos. If we wanted more privacy, sometimes we'd have "road parties" where those carloads of beer-loving teens would drive deep into the rural roads where nobody lived, surrounded by farmland and ditches for miles, and drink and smoke and blast music under the stars.

This particular night I was awkwardly flirting with the chestnut-haired center of the girls' basketball team, whom I'd had a long-running crush on. Just as I was telling a joke about Spanish class, the red and blue lights of Deshler's only policeman lit up behind me. All the beer-drinking kids scattered and drove off, but my friend Terry and I, who weren't drinking, got caught and charged with loitering and breaking the town curfew.

This was, thankfully, the end of my lawless streak, and I would be surprised if anyone outside of my immediate family even remembers the incident. However, it's surprising *The Story of the Great Black Swamp* doesn't mention Harry Pierpont or Simon Girty, because this film proves that it has a real love of the macabre. Maybe Glenn just had too many other highlights to hit after burying the viewer alive during the opening credits?

The next time we see our lanky host, he appears to be casually chilling out beside a corncrib, explaining how this area was carved into a lake by a massive glacier that melted twenty million years ago. The lake eventually receded and left behind a thick yellow clay that refused to drain properly, creating a nightmarish 1,500 square miles of standing water that became the Great Black Swamp. Maybe oblivious to the Girty story, Glenn claims that nobody—Native American or pioneer—was ever bold enough to even attempt to live within its borders until the early nineteenth century.

"Those people who happened, for one reason or another, to venture into the swamp gave it a dirty name, telling horror story after horror story and swearing they'd never go back," Glenn says, walking through a row of waving green soybean leaves. Our cheerful guide pauses, and his tone unexpectedly shifts into Vincent Price mode. "Stories about biting flies and mosquitoes that left the horses ribboned with blood and the riders driven mad with welts and itching. Stories about getting lost almost immediately in the dark woods and trying to find one's way out. About the black oozing mud that seemed to have no bottom, creating fears that people would sink out of sight in one of those *devil's holes*."

Pioneer George W. Perky noted, "We read that God divided the land from the water, but here is a place He forgot." The swamp was dense and cruel to an almost mythical degree. A hunter once got lost for three days outside Fort Meigs, near Toledo. According to records, he wandered among the trees and wolves until he accidentally walked into the fort's walls, at which point he did not recognize his wife or children or even know his name. Future president and Ohio native William Henry Harrison said a couple of trips across the Black Swamp could kill a brigade of packhorses.

When not battling mud and mosquitoes, travelers were overwhelmed by wildlife. One early 1800s report noted: "In hollow trees live bears, raccoons, opossums, and wildcats in great numbers. Troops of small deer sprang across our path more than once, and we heard the gobbling of wild turkeys. Eagles and hawks and a colorful variety of songbirds, some attired in the most magnificent plumage, nest in its branches," he wrote, adding that the dark water was stocked with turtles, black snakes, and fish, including pike, pickerel, sturgeon, white and black bass, muskellunge, and other varieties that all "rose in clumsy heaps." Heaps so plentiful that a different explorer claimed the violent thrashing of all the jumping fish in the Maumee River spooked his horse. An 1813 issue of the *Weekly Register of Baltimore* noted, "The quantity of fish taken at this place is most surprising. Some days there are not less than 1000 or 1500 taken with the hook." Another explorer claimed he caught eleven catfish in one day, many being so large that he was able to run his fist down their throats.

If it weren't enough that something seemed to be trying to kill a man at every step during daylight hours, darkness was far more dangerous. One explorer said his entire party was overtaken by "a malicious swamp demon or by mere anxiety about the approaching night." Another was too terrified to set up camp and rowed a boat through the pitch-black night, describing how "the dark woods rose without interruption on both sides. Only a narrow strip of dark grey sky kept us from thinking we were travelling through a cave; it required no very lively imagination to compare ourselves to the souls sailing down the rivers of Hades."

Some people simply vanished, like blacksmith Jacob Nofziger, who went into the swamp never to be seen again.

Tilly Buttrick, who explored America's western frontier on foot between 1818 and 1819, dedicated a lot of writing space to the terrors inflicted by a pack of Black Swamp wolves perched just outside the bucking firelight of their camp, growling and howling and waiting for an opportunity to play Little Red Riding Hood with Buttrick's crew.

Even Charles Dickens, famed British author of *Oliver Twist*, did not find a single thing to celebrate when he encountered Northwest

Ohio. An 1842 nationwide book tour forced Dickens to brave the outskirts of the swamp in order to travel from Cincinnati to Toledo, where he was scheduled to catch a steamship to Buffalo. He briefly wrote about the journey in *American Notes*, mostly a review of the inn where he slept. Dickens said he found the Black Swamp "sluggish and uninteresting enough." In a letter to friend John Forster, Dickens added, "The demeanour in these country parts is invariably morose, sullen, clownish, and repulsive. I should not think on the face of the Earth a people so destitute of humor, vivacity, or the capacity for enjoyment."

As reports filtered back to the East, this portion of the western frontier began to gain a reputation as a no-man's-land to be avoided at all costs. It was not uncommon to find poems written about the Great Black Swamp printed in newspapers. One epic verse about deadly water and wildlife, "From the Old Time and New," imagined a Black Swamp physician's struggles to perform a simple house call:

> The doctor behind him fastened a boat,
> A life-preserver tied round his throat,
> And with rubber pants and vest and coat,
> He was ready to ride, or row, or float!
> If an old she-bear didn't cross his way,
> Or a catamount "chaw him up" for prey,
> He would reach the house by break of day,
> And on the road home would whistle for pay!

The most clearly rendered account of the Great Black Swamp's horrors came from Julius Hermann Moritz Busch. While the German journalist would eventually gain fame as Otto von Bismarck's press agent, Busch began as a newspaper reporter and travel writer. In 1851, Busch got lost in the swamp for a week as he tried to cut across Ohio to interview the polygamous Mormon prophet, pirate, and conman James Strang up around the northern reaches of Lake Michigan.

Busch's report began in the hamlet of Carey, when shortly outside the town limits he was "closed in by nature" and was almost immediately bitten by a copperhead. A schoolmaster traveling with Busch's party gave him some pioneer medical advice for snakebites: "The surest help was to drink, immediately after the injury, as much whiskey as one could procure and to continue with this until the swelling of the injured limb went down."

Like Glenn noted, aside from treasonous, swashbuckling Johnny Depp lookalikes, almost nobody lived inside the swamp's boundaries, and when Busch did find castoff settlers, often encamped on sand ridges, he suggested they were three decades behind the rest of the world. "I believe that their occupants live a life like the worms in the head of cabbage."

It was as if the swamp itself was successfully fighting off all settlement and progress. But it wasn't for lack of trying. Soon, despite the swamp's reputation, the most brilliant minds in the country would set out to destroy the swamp thanks to two places that seemingly had nothing to do with Northwest Ohio: New York and Chicago.

11
THE WORST ROAD IN AMERICA

Disasters do not happen overnight.

And rarely do they have a single source to blame for all their destruction. Rather, disasters are often the product of long stretches of negligence and bad decisions and optimistic best intentions that coalesce in a single catastrophic moment. In most cases, we don't see those elements combining, or if we do, the alarms they set off tend to get overlooked in favor of normalcy.

Case in point: the disastrous settlement of the Great Black Swamp. It was a giant mess that kept getting worse for almost one hundred years before it got better, and its period of "better" would eventually lead to another disaster, the 2014 algae crisis.

The disasters begin with an 1830 roadway project. Up until then, the world at large seemed content to ignore Northwest Ohio. All one million acres of dark, deadly, impenetrable swamp may have remained an explorer's curiosity if not for a city almost 250 miles away. Right as Chicago grew into the biggest, most important metropolis in the Midwest, the Great Black Swamp developed a big target on its back. Traders, travelers, and immigrants moving between New York City and the Windy City were losing time and money because of Ohio's nightmarish upper left atrium. Pull out a map and notice how a straight line could practically be drawn between the two cities, except for Northwest Ohio.

Back in the early 1800s, wise travelers simply went around the Great Black Swamp. Those with a death wish tried to cut directly through Satan's Backyard. Either route added days, or even weeks, to the trip. But only one could get you eaten by a wolf. So there was that.

However, America was in the midst of a Manifest Destiny conquering spree, which made Northwest Ohio seem like a simple equation to solve. This Buckeye State blight was standing in the way of progress, and *nothing* stood in the way of progress in the 1800s. Money was being lost! Worse yet, opportunities to make *more* money were going unfulfilled. This stupid swamp was sandbagging America's greatness, and that would not do.

Since the Louisiana Purchase in 1803, the same year Ohio achieved statehood, the country had been throttling steadily westward, not just exploring but taming its wild plains, rivers, mountains, and deserts. Nature or Natives be damned. So, it seemed almost like an afterthought that America would soon bury this meaningless Ohio mud puddle. The Great Black Swamp was no match for our young nation's optimism and energy!

The prevailing logic of the era said it would be a cinch: Just slice a path through Northwest Ohio connecting New York to Chicago. This would not just be some dinky roadway but the latest, greatest money chute America had ever concocted. This thoroughfare would be an unfettered pipeline sending riches in both directions. Plus, it would lift this backwater part of the country into something respectable and normal.

Recall how, after years of lopsided treaties and bloodshed, Native tribes had been pushed off their ancestral property and forced to take ownership of the Great Black Swamp. In a move both predictable and depressing, the government suddenly decided to take back what it previously determined was worthless, telling tribal leaders in essence, "You can still keep the parts we think are shitty. We just want this *slightly* less shitty section right here," and ran a greasy finger through the gut of the Black Swamp.

By 1808, Ohio Senator John E. Hunt had led the purchase of a thirty-five-mile ribbon of Great Black Swamp for $30,000. The plan was to create a nineteenth-century Ohio autobahn named the Maumee and Western Reserve Road. Speculators claimed great cities would spill outward along the road's path. Others touted the region's inevitable rise as an agricultural superpower—"The Garden of Ohio," several publications predicted.

Construction didn't truly begin until 1823. The first problem was getting rid of all those worthless trees—and hungry wolves and endless pits of mud. And yes, those malaria-filled clouds of mosquitoes should probably scram, too. No worry. America had grit and optimism on its side. Slowly, a 120-foot-wide path was carved through the swamp. All along the route, thousands of trees were left discarded in the crew's wake and simply set ablaze. The tar-black smoke of progress must have filled the skies above Northwest Ohio for months, which left a crude roadbed of ash and charcoal behind. Shallow drainage ditches were dug along both sides of the turnpike.

Horses and coaches would begin smoothly cruising east and west very shortly.

The Maumee and Western Reserve Road was finally finished in 1827 and quickly lived up to expectations. The road saw an immediate swell of traffic, at least 5,500 travelers in one year alone, which is an absolute explosion for such a desolate region. The government's vision for the primitive superhighway was, by early accounts, a huge success.

As predicted, previously unsellable land near the road began to be snapped up with the intention of clearing and settling it. Thirty-one taverns were built along the thirty-one-mile route. One such speculator was a Columbus, Ohio banker named David Deshler who purchased thousands of acres far south of the road, deep into no-man's-land, and then sat on that worthless property, waiting for an opportunity to arrive.

Today, you can still find evidence of this doomed Maumee and Western Reserve Road construction project ten miles outside of Toledo, in Perrysburg. It doesn't look like anything special today. It looks like the suburbs, a really cute suburb with a historic Main Street filled with charming brick buildings, bustling coffee shops, bakeries, salons, and restaurants, including the perfectly named "Perrysburgers." Today, it's an upper-middle-class bedroom community with treelined streets and charming Victorian homes. More than likely, folks here commute into Toledo for work, and more than likely, they don't realize their finely paved State Route 20 was, for a time, considered the biggest mess in American civil engineering history.

The only remains of Perrysburg's section of the Maumee and Western Reserve Road is a triangle-shaped park about the size of a studio apartment. The park butts right up against all four lanes of

Route 20, buzzing with bass-heavy stereos and the occasional semi-truck. The heart of the park is a small limestone pillar, on which the writing has eroded like an old gravestone. This is a mile marker for the Maumee and Western Reserve Road, and if you saw one of these back in the 1830s, it was a sign that you were probably having the worst day of your life.

Even though humans were slowly filtering in, the Black Swamp's wolves were still fearless predators intent on defending their home. Fourteen-year-old Pony Express rider John S. Butler documented a time when an entire pack stalked him and a friend. They were forced to beat the wolves off with sticks only to have the rest of the snarling pack follow and attack through the night until they found a tavern for shelter. Others reported sleeping beneath an overturned wagon only to have its sideboards eaten away by the aggressive creatures. The wolves, it turned out, were just getting started.

However, a far more immediate problem was the road itself. The Maumee and Western Reserve's popularity led to quick deterioration. Soon, it had acquired a national reputation of its own.

"You could hardly call it a road," Glenn says in *The Story of the Great Black Swamp*, as the film shifts to sepia-toned photos of horses and carriages navigating what look to be remnants of World War I battlefields, but are, in fact, Northwest Ohio. "By 1835 the quagmire had come to be known as the worst piece of road on the continent." The Maumee and Western was virtually impassable.

The area tavern owners must have known this would happen, because during the muddy season a traveler could slog forward only about a mile each day, roughly about the distance between each tavern.

Some weary travelers reportedly left their tavern at sunrise only to return to that same spot at sunset. "Within the first mile," a 1966 *Toledo Blade* retrospective noted, "his wagon might have been sucked down into the mud and it would take the rest of the day to get it out."

One Michigan-bound settler ended up paying over $100 (roughly $3,500 today) to get his horse and wagon out of several mudholes. "He was still far from Perrysburg and he had no more cash," authors Kathryn and Gordon Keller noted. "So he pulled up to the next mudhole, and there he quickly recouped his fortune by helping and collecting from other settlers slogging through."

These taverns were sometimes little more than crude log cabins that, along with a place to sleep, would provide meals of racoon, possum, deer, or wild turkey—whatever the owner could shoot that day. A tavern's meager grain crops provided feed for oxen and horses. Historian Nan Card notes, "Warm fires and the ever-present whiskey jug made the mud, cold, and back-breaking misery almost bearable. At dusk, the taverns filled up quickly. Every available inch of space would be filled with exhausted families wrapped in mud-caked, damp blankets. Many were forced to sleep in their wagons or beside campfires."

Mudholes were a major issue, and unverified accounts claim more than one person reported almost losing an entire horse in one. Nan Card points out that some travelers swore some mudholes' depths "could only be measured by a ten-foot pole." Tavern owners often made more money from pulling people from the mud than from innkeeping. Some were accused of watering the holes in front of their inns to bog down travelers so they'd be forced to stay the night. According to historian Prudence Dangler, "One tavern-keeper who had a particularly fine mudhole decided to leave the country. When he sold his business, he drew up a quit-claim and sold it for five dollars to a neighbor," thus creating the nation's first mudhole franchise.

When Charles Dickens skirted the Black Swamp, his editor G.W. Putnam was also along for the journey. Putnam's account of the trip, later published in *The Atlantic*, described traveling through the swamp in greater detail than his literary-celebrity companion's. Though we don't know whether they were specifically on the Maumee and Western Reserve Road, his diary mentions traveling through an unbroken forest in Northern Ohio, just outside of Toledo, and also notes that it looked like a "wild and uncivilized territory." Also, the road they traveled on sounds mighty familiar: "Holes nearly large enough to bury coach, horses, and all were constantly occurring," Putnam wrote. "The driver managed with great skill to avoid them. It was a wondrous talent that put the wood and iron of that coach together, for it did not seem possible that it could long remain unbroken."

Attempts at road improvement included corduroying the path by sinking logs into the mud until they hit bottom, and then stacking log atop log until a bumpy, ridged pathway (much like the texture of the fabric) emerged from the sludge. Most of the mud just absorbed logs as if it were bottomless. Half a century later, when an official road was finally built, engineers discovered perfectly preserved logs buried dozens of feet belowground. In some places, where the bedrock was near the surface, corduroyed roads did appear, which, oddly, made things worse sometimes. Dickens said a corduroyed road "is like nothing but going up a steep flight of stairs in an omnibus."

"Mrs. Dickens had the back seat to herself; as the terrible jolting increased," Putman wrote about his party transitioning from mudholes to corduroyed roads. "Mr. Dickens, taking two handkerchiefs, tied the ends of them to the door-posts on each side, and the other ends Mrs. Dickens wound around her wrists and hands. This contrivance, to which was added the utmost bracing of the feet, enabled the kind and patient lady to endure the torture of the 'corduroy.'

"Mr. Dickens on his side, and I on mine, kept a sharp lookout ahead as well as we could, and when we saw—as we did almost every minute—an uncommonly large hole into which the wheels *must* go, we shouted, 'Corduroy!' and prepared ourselves for the shock. But preparation was of little avail, for with all our strength we found it impossible to keep our places, but were constantly tumbling upon each other and picking ourselves up from the bottom of the coach. At last we got through the swamp, and thankfully left the 'corduroy' behind us."

Like Wile E. Coyote sitting down to a drafting table full of blueprints just after plummeting off a cliff, the brightest engineering minds of the era continued focusing their energy on the Great Black Swamp despite these failures. By 1850, builders asked: What's the swamp's greatest defense? The answer they came up with was its impossibly dense tree coverage. (Not the bottomless mud pits or malaria, or, you know, murderous wolves. But we'll let them have this one.) Thus, Ohio's roadway engineers decided that they would just use the Great Black Swamp's strengths against it like some kind of ecological tae kwon do match. Soon, an army of sawyers began slicing the land's plentiful trees into planks and laying them into a smooth boardwalk along the Maumee and Western's path. To everyone's delight, this tactic actually worked.

Just about the time people got ready to celebrate, travelers found that this roadway was wide enough for only one wagon, so when meeting oncoming traffic, someone had to pull over—which inevitably left them stuck in the mud. Adding to the headaches, those planks began floating away during the first serious rains of the season. The boardwalk effort was abandoned after less than a decade, leaving the Maumee and Western Reserve Road in worse shape than ever.

Cut back to *The Story of the Great Black Swamp*. Glenn, in his nifty double-knit slacks, stands beneath a small bridge with a sad little Northwest Ohio creek running by his feet. You can find these puny streams all over the area. They have no plant or animal life, and their trickle of Yoo-hoo-colored water tends to transport only Styrofoam cups and candy wrappers from one end of town to the other, especially back in Glenn's pre-recycling era. Prior to living in Oregon in the early 2000s, I thought this was what normal looked like everywhere, before learning creeks and rivers were not meant to be liquid dumpsters and that natural bodies of water are often clear—with fish living in them!

"A similar attempt to get over the swamp if one couldn't get through it was made by the Ohio Railroad Company in the 1830s and 1840s," says Glenn. The camera continues its slow zoom out, and surprise, Glenn has been standing beneath a rusted iron railroad bridge this whole time. I understand where he's going with this one.

This was the *Industrial Age!* There was no place on Earth where tracks hadn't been laid. No mountain or tundra or desert where steam engines couldn't plow forward. Manifest Destiny, ahoy!

Once again, humans used the swamp's own trees as weapons. The railroad planned to build a long, elevated train bridge from Sandusky City to Maumee Bay, hovering above its muck and hungry wolves via a series of trestles. The job required a steampunk-looking contraption that was essentially a train engine that featured a buzzsaw at the end of a long mechanical arm. The idea was that this cartoonish machine would cut down trees and feed those logs back to a traveling sawmill that followed the buzzsaw, which instantly converted this fresh wood into the trestles and rail ties that would then be built in its wake.

A weekly paper in Toledo at the time wrote: "It is wonderful and marvelous to see such a thing of wood and iron and fire and water, walking deliberately and safely, and almost intellectually, over the deep morasses of the Black Swamp, apparently by its own volition, making its own road as it passes." Optimistically, this writer guessed that "nine months will enable us to travel the far-famed Black Swamp in less than two hours."

Not bad, reducing a thirty-one-day trek through Hell down to a pleasant couple of hours. This, surely, would end the Great Black Swamp's reign of terror.

Glenn steps up from that nasty creek bed and onto some train tracks. Directly behind our host is my personal Golden Gate Bridge, Statue of Liberty, and Epcot Center all rolled into one. For a fragment of the film, I spot the most recognizable monument of my hometown: a mint green water tower with *DESHLER* painted in huge black letters across its face.

Prior to watching *The Story of the Great Black Swamp*, I had never seen my hometown on television. If discovering a whole documentary had been made about Northwest Ohio was a surprise, seeing Deshler onscreen is a stunner. I didn't even know a professional camera crew had ever set foot within the city limits. Forty years later, it's still thrilling, magical, and unexpected.

In the Jerome Library's AV room, a huge, glowing smile appears on my face as I remember that I have stood beneath that same water tower as Glenn. He's right beside the town reservoir, the largest body of water for twenty miles in every direction, the place where, while on summer break, my friends and I would ditch our bikes and run along the tracks to yell "Water!" to train engineers as their giant diesel engines puttered past. More often than not, an itty-bitty six-pack of waters flew from the open window—barrel-shaped plastic bottles with pull-off aluminum foil lids that looked like the corn-syrupy Kool-Aid knockoffs "Little Hugs," but the liquid was crystal clear. We'd all have a gleeful gulp, not because we were thirsty, but because in 1980s Northwest Ohio we'd never seen bottled water before.

When I refocus on Glenn, he's describing how this Black Swamp railway endeavor quickly went all to hell. If you guessed metric tons of wooden trestles and steel tracks were spaghetti-slurped into the swamp, you are officially smarter than an 1800s railroad magnate. Bravo! The film plasters up embarrassing photos of buried tracks poking from the mud like a sunken xylophone. "By 1845, the Ohio Railroad Company was bankrupt," Glenn says. "The swamp had won again."

12
A FUNERAL EVERY DAY

In 1835, around the same year that the Maumee and Western Reserve Road was first completed, a cartographic quirk made a thin sliver of land, which included Toledo, seemingly belong to both Ohio and Michigan, depending on the map. "Ohio wanted the Toledo Strip for development purposes, ignoring the presence of the Great Black Swamp in the northwest portion of the state, which was believed by many to be the natural barrier between Ohio and Michigan," historian John H. Doyle recounted in 1919. "Michigan wanted to prevent development of the Strip because any commercial center there would rival Detroit." There were probably some diplomatic talks, but it didn't take long before twenty-three-year-old Michigan Governor Stevens T. Mason sent a militia to Toledo to claim the city for his state, threatening their neighbors to the south by saying: "We promise you hospitable graves."

The governor of Ohio sent nobody.

It wasn't that the Buckeye State didn't *try* to send fighters, it's just that the army from Columbus got stuck in the Great Black Swamp.

Soldiers and weapons were bogged down and "shaken to pieces by the fever and ague of the Black Swamp," according to the *Detroit Free Press*. By the time they dragged themselves through the thickets and muck, the US government had already stepped in and awarded Toledo to Ohio. Michigan won the Upper Peninsula as a consolation prize. The Toledo War, as the book I picked up at the National Museum of the Great Lakes tells me, barely ever even happened, but it made a significant impact on the future.

After this miserable experience, Ohio Governor Robert Lucas made the first true efforts to kill the swamp by pouring more money into the Maumee and Western Reserve Road. "In 1839, legislation was passed to macadamize and drain the road, making it fit for heavy travel," Glenn says in *The Story of the Great Black Swamp*. "The engineers who redesigned the road figured out that the old design was causing the mudholes."

Experts took a closer look and discovered the previous attempts at the Black Swamp superhighway didn't take into consideration that the land gently slopes toward Lake Erie. Its ditches had been built in a backward configuration that actually dammed up water, flooding the road. New ditches were built in a manner that shuffled the water away, including culverts that allowed drainage to pass beneath roadways. In short order, all that useless muddy water vanished into Lake Erie, never to be thought of again. Things were looking up, and optimism had never been higher in this portion of the young state.

"People began to recognize that this improved method of building the road not only kept the road useable, but drained the surrounding area and made it *inhabitable*." Glenn says *inhabitable* with total, adorable wonder. That's dramatic range! Lest you forget, this man's acting skills once convinced the moviegoing public that he had been beaten to death with a prosthetic limb by Academy Award winner Timothy Hutton.

According to my math, inhabitable = normal, so now that Northwest Ohio was finally getting normal it was never looking back. Farmers snapped up semidry land, land still densely packed with timber, as it hit the market, cheap at about five dollars an acre.

Garden of Ohio, here we come.

"They were really naive people, innocents who had no idea what they were getting themselves into," says Glenn. "Probably if they'd known, they'd never have come."

It sounds impossible, but this new and improved period of Black Swamp settlement was actually more miserable than its days as the primeval, bloodthirsty rivers of Hades.

For starters, the swamp's original alpha inhabitants weren't in a hurry to leave just because some humans moved into the neighborhood. Massive wolf packs treated settlers' livestock like an all-you-can-eat buffet. And when they were picking their teeth after devouring goats and sheep, the wolves were so aggressive they were known to paw and growl at the doors of rustic cabins. Those who could not afford a door hoped to scare away the creatures by lighting massively bright fires in their hearths. Sometimes it worked, but some settlers wrote of wolves spending the entire night punching their snouts through floorboards and wall gaps, like some kind of fur-covered Jack Nicholson in a pioneer version of *The Shining*.

However, wolves were only a small fraction of what was punishing newcomers. "The settlers were literally stung out of their senses by horseflies, gnats, and mosquitoes," Glenn says in that sweetly disarming grandpa voice. "Why, the horseflies were as big as bumblebees and could almost knock a person down with their stings. And the gnats and mosquitoes came by the millions, sometimes in clouds."

The screen flashes with daguerreotypes of horses walking down roads and plowing fields while draped in heavy white canvas blankets in a weak attempt at keeping the animals from bleeding to death from bug bites. The settlers themselves weren't much better off, forced to wear long sleeves and gloves even in the summer, veiling their faces with kerchiefs just to be outside.

Cases of malaria skyrocketed.

I am reminded of Melanie Coulter's bear grease advice. Since the swamp and forest were shrinking so rapidly, bears were likely displaced and easier to hunt. The resourceful Midwesterner in me thinks that's a pretty great lemons-to-lemonade story, but the part of me that likes bears is depressed.

"The only other defense was a smudge pot." Glenn picks up a cast-iron kettle about the size of a pumpkin, gray smoke petering from its spout. The smoldering wood inside drove away insects. Glen tells us swamp folks carried these while tending to the animals, stuffed them under the table at dinner, and kept them beside the bed at night. The smudge pots' low-hanging haze was everywhere, and one writer compared settlers to "so many hams in a smokehouse." This may be the first instance of Northwest Ohioans stoically suffering. Our original shrug, and smile, and back to normal moment.

Water, big shock, was also the source of much Black Swamp settler misery. Considering how Northwest Ohio had gone from six feet of sludge to merely being coated in a few inches of standing water, you'd think there would be a lot of drinking options. Just like opening the taps in Toledo during the algae crisis 150 years in the future, you could *technically* drink the water in the swamp, it was just a suicidal idea. Many settlers filled tankards in shallow trenches filled with filthy groundwater, while others simply lifted up a floorboard of their cabin and dragged a pail through the standing water.

Cholera levels skyrocketed.

By this point, thousands of settlers now lived in the Great Black Swamp, and it was kinda sorta better than before—but survival remained difficult. With malaria and cholera rates spiking, death was a constant part of this early era. Poetry, once again, was a preferred medium to communicate hardship, such as this dark ode found in the *Maumee City Express*, which laid bare that people were dying at such an alarming rate there often wasn't time for a proper Christian burial.

> There's a funeral every day
> Without a hearse or pall;
> They tuck them in the ground
> With breeches, coat, and all.

This poem doesn't even touch on the darkest part of Black Swamp death. Several reports claimed that freshly dug graves would fill with water before the bodies could even be lowered, or that if a casket did get successfully put underground, the water table would simply push the deceased up through the mud, leaving wild animals to tear apart the body.

I can't help but wonder while sifting through info like this, *Who were these people?* Even that poem was uncredited. There is very little biographical information about these early settlers. Even *The Story of the Great Black Swamp* pretty much avoids mentioning anyone specific by name. And when they are mentioned in the historic record, little background info is given beyond where they were born and when.

Who is the Great Black Swamp's Daniel Boone? Its Sacagawea? This blooper reel of settlers getting clobbered by the swamp seemingly has no heroes, no villains, not even a Falstaff to laugh at. Rather, to explore Black Swamp history is to learn about *event* after *event* after *event*.

But let's not dwell on how Northwest Ohio seems incapable of or unwilling to specifically take credit for anything. Because, believe it or not, this is actually the turning point for the swamp. Just as life in Northwest Ohio seemed like it was at its darkest, this is the precise moment when the comeback of a lifetime begins. We're on the cusp of the Great Black Swamp's next act, the truly American part of the story where a lightbulb goes off and nature finally gets its ass kicked.

13
TOO MANY FROGS, TOO MANY MUDHOLES

My hometown captures this turning point well and represents hundreds of similar Northwest Ohio towns as they each pulled themselves from living like worms in the head of a cabbage toward prosperity—and, eventually, twenty-first-century toxic algae.

Deshler, technically categorized as a village, ranks as the 538th largest municipality in the state by population. The former Great Black Swamp is now made up of dozens of towns like Deshler, similarly low-ranked dots on the map that are home to anywhere from a couple thousand to a couple dozen people. Towns like Hamler, Holgate, Risingsun, Jerry City, Grelton, Liberty Center, West Unity, North Baltimore, and the curiously named Mount Cory (elevation 814 feet. For comparison, Deshler's elevation is only 100 feet lower).

Like most of these tiny communities, Deshler is not large enough to be the county seat of Henry County. Today, that honor goes to the far bigger Napoleon, which boasts a population of almost nine thousand and offers exotic things like Walmart, Taco Bell, and radio station WNDH, whose morning DJ, when I was a child, would wish you a happy birthday if you sent in a postcard with your name and birthdate. Here in Appalachia, I terrify my son and students when they claim to live in the middle of nowhere. I tell them, no, living in the middle of nowhere means driving thirty minutes to the nearest Taco Bell in Napoleon like I had to as a young man.

Henry County is shaped like Utah, if Utah's panhandle doglegged to the west instead of jutting north. Deshler is in the bottom righthand corner of the county. Henry County is fractured into thirteen townships, and Deshler's township, Bartlow, was the final township settled in the entire state, which must mean it was the most isolated and inhospitable section of the Great Black Swamp—which pretty much made it one of the most unlivable parts of America, if not the world, at the time.

Prior to 1860, there is not much information on the area. One historian noted that the only sound that greeted the ears of the early settler was either the moaning of the huge trees under the pressure of hard winds, the yelping of some wild animal, or the crack of the hunter's gun. That was when there actually were any humans around. By 1860, pockets of the Black Swamp were being slowly settled, but Bartlow Township, the absolute center of the swamp, was still so empty that it only had four tax-paying residents.

It might have stayed wild and moaning if not for two things around that time: First, massive hand-dug ditches, like the ones on the Maumee and Western road, aided the natural drainage of the land. Second, after this rudimentary early drainage, the Dayton and Michigan Railroad cut a path just wide enough for a north–south train line. Right where the Great Black Swamp was darkest in Bartlow Township was also about where the steam engines would run out of water, stranding the entire rig in the wilderness unless its pressure tanks could be refilled. Thus, the rail company excavated a small reservoir at a perilously waterlogged spot. Soon, they added a makeshift office built from a decommissioned boxcar, allowing engineers a place to switch and rest.

This was the exact place where Glenn stood beside the Deshler water tower in *The Story of the Great Black Swamp* and where I scored free train water as a kid.

About this same time, a Columbus lawyer and Civil War veteran named John Deshler returned to Ohio after a failed stint as a legislator in Buffalo, New York. His father, David Deshler, had been one of those eager speculators in the 1830s after the Maumee and Western Reserve Road was built, snapping up large tracts of worthless swamp and simply sitting on the property in hopes *something* would happen. When David Deshler died, John took over the family business and inherited ten thousand acres of wolf-ridden, mud-soaked, malaria-poisoned lower Henry County. Aiming to make something of this investment, and perhaps make a name for himself after that botched attempt at New York politics, John Deshler began encouraging development around that lonely boxcar and reservoir.

By 1865, that area had grown to include a log cabin hotel called the Phoenix House, several sawmills, a train station, and, apparently, an absurd number of amphibians. John Deshler originally named the place Alma, after his grandniece. Alma Deshler was sixteen at the time, and Uncle John brought her north to see the place. According to historians, "She was jumping from log to log, when her uncle asked her what she thought of her namesake as a town. She replied,

'Too much water, too many frogs and mudholes. Why don't you call it *Deshler*?'"

So, John begrudgingly renamed the depressing Black Swamp town after himself. It must have felt like a punishment. Down in Columbus, his father's name was etched onto tony hotels and banks, but a little girl forced him to lend the prestigious family moniker to such a wet, lifeless, unimportant place.

This little railroad stopover would have surely died had John not received an inside tip that the Baltimore and Ohio Railroad was looking to construct an east–west line through the swamp to better connect New York and Chicago. In a desperate effort to resuscitate this mudhole, he offered the B&O free land, knowing the rail line crossroads would skyrocket the value of his worthless property. The railroad accepted, and a lively, productive town was born.

Only fifteen months after the B&O line opened, the town was, as one historian noted, "growing much as a mushroom grows. Spreading itself over the refuse and decay." Hammering and sawing filled the quiet lulls between train whistles as businesses began opening rapidly, including several stores, churches, a school, two hotels, a sawmill, and some small timber businesses. The town's population boomed from four to four hundred.

Despite this 9,900 percent population swing, Deshler had stalled somewhat by 1880. Homes and farm plots were not in great demand because the land was still very waterlogged. The United Methodist Church was so bad that congregants frequently had to wade knee deep through water to attend Sunday service. Main Street consisted of a hastily built corduroy road that would have given Charles Dickens a heart attack. Mosquitoes filled the air, and stray pigs roamed at will, often basking in the heat of the furnace of Albert Suber's foundry. Perhaps playing off of this sight, the Ross House Hotel erected a sign featuring an old sow with a litter of pigs that read, "Warm Meals at All Hours."

For thirty-five years, that constant layer of water prohibited serious settlement in Deshler and countless other towns like it in Northwest Ohio. There's no telling how many people were driven away by these wretched conditions. It's not crazy to assume the ones who were brave enough to stay looked around and thought, "*This* is what we fought so hard for?"

But amid this scrappy pioneer population was a stranger who'd recently moved to Deshler from Bowling Green. James B. Hill would soon become the Great Black Swamp's hero, villain, and Falstaff all rolled into one.

14

THE BUCKEYE TRACTION DITCHER

James B. Hill should be patron saint of Northwest Ohio—or at least patron saint of this story. He invented a machine called the Buckeye Traction Ditcher, and he checks all my boxes.

Hill is our hero: His invention drained the swamp in a matter of years, leading to its complete settlement shortly thereafter. He brought the normalcy we see today.

Hill is our villain: His invention drained the swamp in a matter of years and killed practically all its native plant and animal life, which directly led to Toledo's 2014 toxic algae outbreak. Plus, I find an unattributed mention of a John Henry–esque battle up in Canada between Hill's ditcher and a fifty-man digging crew, in which the machine lays waste to the men, essentially wiping out an entire industry.

Hill is also our Falstaff: His invention drained the swamp in a matter of years, and it made him such a rich man he felt empowered to write a silly autobiography. I get my hands on a poorly Xeroxed PDF of Hill's unpublished book. To my disappointment, it's probably about what you'd expect from a high school dropout/ditch digger/industrial magnate. The most entertaining thing about the manuscript is his mildly humorous quirk of repeatedly asking the fairies on his shoulders for advice at crucial moments in his life.

Beyond that, there's not much to go on. The man has left a very faint legacy behind. This is no attention-seeking titan of industry like Henry Ford or Steve Jobs (self-indulgent autobiography notwithstanding). Hill proves to be maybe the most Northwest Ohio of all heroes and villains—one who does not draw too much attention to himself.

James B. Hill bounced around Northwest Ohio after dropping out of school. In 1882, he was doing labor for a farmer and tried his hand at manually digging trenches and laying drainage tiles. Soon he had a reputation as the best tiler in Northwest Ohio. By 1892, he had begun working in a machine shop in Bowling Green, staying nights and weekends to work on his own invention, which he built without drawings or blueprints, instead making all the patterns by carving wood with a jackknife. In 1893, he sold a prototype of an automated ditch-digging machine for $700. At the exact moment his business took off, a national depression hit, and the machine shop went into receivership. Hill found a more affordable shop in Deshler and produced five ditchers there before moving again, to Carey, where business finally boomed and the Great Black Swamp was forever changed.

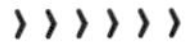

I drive to Carey, Ohio, one rainy afternoon to see if there is any trace left of Hill's empire. Carey is about twice the size of Deshler yet offers residents about the same amenities: a few gas stations, a pizza joint, some beauty shops, and a hardware store. I have seen a hundred towns just like it in the area.

The steady downpour makes the roof of my car sound like it is sizzling. This storm hasn't let up since last night, so the streets and most yards are now rippling with water. There is no historical marker for Hill's Buckeye Traction Ditcher. His workshop, if it is still standing, isn't noted. There does not even appear to be a street named after the city's most fascinating resident. Nobody I spoke with had even ever heard of James B. Hill. Perhaps that's because Hill is steeply overshadowed by the town's Catholic church.

Specifically, by a miraculous event that reportedly happened long before Hill migrated to the town. On May 25, 1875, an overcast gray day not much different than the gloomy morning I visit Carey, the church was holding a processional parade to transport a small statue, *Our Lady of Consolation*. The wooden sculpture of a proud-faced Mary and an infant Jesus had been carved in Luxembourg and was on the final few miles of its journey to its new home in Carey.

Reports say a procession of hundreds of parishioners, including Father Joseph Peter Gloden and a troop of young girls in black veils, began to carry the statue down the road. Midway through the seven-mile sojourn, the clouds turned the color of ash, the bodies of every marcher shook with thunder, and blue shreds of lightning ripped across the sky. According to the church, "After the procession had begun the area was inundated by heavy rains from a severe storm. While it rained and stormed before, behind, and on all sides of the procession, neither the statue of Our Lady of Consolation nor anyone in the procession suffered one drop of rain."

Since then, people have been coming to Carey with all sorts of ailments, claiming the statue has healing powers. By 1917, nearly sixty people had said that their maladies—including deafness, curvature of the spine, paralysis, and even one little girl whose left eye was gouged out with a steel pen—were cured after a visit to *Our Lady of Consolation*. For decades, pilgrims returned, often in search of similar healing. The site was so popular that a 1995 article appeared in the supermarket tabloid *National Examiner* under the headline "Miracles of Faith: Cripples Walk...Blind See...Sick Are Healed at Amazing Church."

Today, over twelve thousand visitors come every summer for a two-day festival celebrating the statue. I was raised Catholic and never heard so much as a peep about this faith healing in Woodstock, not thirty minutes from my front door.

I pull up to the Basilica, a squared-off brick structure that seems like any other Northwest Ohio church, and decide to see the statue for myself. Inside, it is far more ornate than I anticipated—a huge, domed ceiling covered in fine murals. I wander a little. My wet shoes echo since I'm the only person in an enormous church. Hundreds of little red prayer candles flicker in the corner. Toward the front of the church is the shrine, the famous statue of Mary and baby Jesus, both dressed in matching purple outfits today.

I pause a moment, wondering if I will feel something supernatural, if my maladies will be healed. Nothing happens. Still, there's something comforting about this place. There is a peace here, a calm, that's hard to ignore.

Outside, I run into a tall, cowled monk named Brother Randy. As the rain speckles my glasses, we chat about the summer festival a little and I ask if he's heard of James B. Hill or the Buckeye Traction Ditcher.

He has not.

››››››

Maybe that's the way Hill wanted it. In a brilliant literary stroke of Midwestern modesty, his memoir spends about one hundred pages talking about life before the most important thing he ever did and then quickly glosses over the major accomplishments. Even the fairies sitting on his shoulder seem to be silent at this crucial juncture. It's as if he is essentially blushing and saying, "Aw, it was no biggie. Anybody could have invented a ditch-digging machine that dragged a swamp the size of Connecticut out of the prehistoric ages and into the twentieth century." And that's kind of where the book ends.

But the Buckeye Traction Ditcher *is* a big deal. Not only did it drain the Great Black Swamp, leading to the construction of tens of thousands of miles of ditches in Ohio alone, but the tread design also became the basis for all military tank technology in World War I. This machine would also go on to be used to drain parts of Africa and the sections of Florida that would someday become Disney World. The American Society of Engineers honored Hill and the ditcher in its Hall of Fame. In 1904, *Scientific American* called him a "mechanical genius."

After my rain-soaked visit to Carey's Basilica, I get a chance to see a Buckeye Traction Ditcher in person at the nearby Hancock County Historical Society. The ditcher looks like the skeleton of some more sleek contraption. In a perfectly Northwest Ohio design stroke, there is no artifice or aerodynamics to its appearance. By contrast, automobiles and trains of the era were becoming sleek and elegant. That year's newest sensation, the Ford Model F, looked like a piece of art with its sprawling white canopy, spoked wheels, and aluminum body covering the engine and doors. The Buckeye Ditcher was not meant to win any hearts with its appearance. A Buckeye Ditcher looks exactly like the thing it is—a ham-fisted working-class machine built by a farmer, created specifically for dirty, difficult work.

Nothing I can think of looks quite like this. The most distinct feature is its eight-foot-tall boiler shaped like a gigantic beer bottle, which breathes plumes of white steam in YouTube videos I've watched. The next thing that sticks out is its unique digging wheel, looking more like a massive iron loom than anything farm related. It is taller than I am and spins without an axle. The wheel operates something like a riverboat paddlewheel, with a number of large, dirt-hauling scoopers affixed to the outside of the wheel, which carves a perfect trench. The body of the machine is long and sparse and sits on four wide steel wheels so that it can roll over swampy ground without sinking. The true stroke of genius is the second half of the machine's job. After the wheel scoops a straight trench, another part of the ditcher drops clay tiles into the ground, creating an instant drainage system for oversaturated fields.

When in action, the Buckeye Ditcher looks like it is going in several directions at once. While its steam engine pistons punch the air, the heart of the machine performs some kind of optical illusion as its four steel wheels creep slowly forward while that digging wheel rotates in the opposite direction, like it is fighting itself, going against the grain of the land, chewing up soil and tossing piles back with each rotation.

Within a few years, James B. Hill singlehandedly did the impossible: he changed the landscape entirely and killed the unkillable Great Black Swamp.

Hill doesn't look like much of a killer, nor does he look like much of a mechanical wizard. In the only photo I can find, on a website dedicated to famous people from Findlay, Ohio, he looks more like a turn-of-the-century candy man: balding, peering out blankly behind round wire-rimmed glasses, sporting an enormous white mustache and a finely pressed suit. His head is tilted toward the camera like he's waiting for a grandchild to give him a hug before forking over some peppermints.

Research turns up zero quotes from the man, except for a newspaper article titled "Grandpa of Tanks Ponders on War" in which he gives precisely ten words, all relating to the Buckeye Ditcher's unintentional inspiration for tank treads. His Wikipedia page boasts about the Buckeye Ditcher and credits him for inventing "Hill's White Cob Yellow Dent" corn seed, a strain specifically suited for growing in Louisiana swampland. Wikipedia also claims that near his death, Hill said he had over one hundred descendants, though that claim is not substantiated in any other research. A distant relative quoted in a Louisiana newspaper in 2018 says Hill did not leave behind any money from his inventions.

By 1902, he had sold the business to the Van Buren, Heck, and Marvin Company, which opened a factory in Findlay and mass-produced the machines. Besides actually seeing one of these machines in person, the other highlight of my visit to the Hancock

County Historical Society is snooping around its archives and coming across some sheet music for "The Buckeye Traction Ditcher March," which was a sort of 1920s-era theme song meant to be played by the factory's volunteer marching band. I do not know how to read music, but I make a copy for the sheer oddball joy that a thing like this exists.

In a matter of years, every farm in Northwest Ohio used the Buckeye Ditcher to drain its land and send the runoff into those V-shaped ditches to the Maumee River, which flowed into Lake Erie. In less than one hundred years, the Department of the Interior would estimate, Ohio's total wetlands went from five million acres to less than half a million. James B. Hill's miracle invention eliminated the Great Black Swamp entirely, except for places like Goll Woods.

15
COME AS YOU ARE

Goll Woods does not look any swampier than my Bell Woods trek with Melanie. However, when you stare up, the tree canopy is dark, nearly black in spots, which is satisfying. The stuffy air is silent except for the piccolo runs of distant birds. Shallow puddles of motionless dark water, shiny as maple syrup, extend so long you lose track of where they end. I breathe in fresh, mulchy smells. The forest is dense with rail straight tulip trees and the ridged bark of buckeye trees (famous for its poisonous nut, which is confusingly also the namesake of a delicious peanut butter and chocolate confection). The floor is thick with the green ribs of Goldie's ferns, glade ferns, lady ferns, and a dozen other types I don't know. Most notable is the unending carpet of saucer-shaped green leaves of garlic mustard, an invasive species that has been choking out native plants for years.

The air is teeming with bugs, though Ryan Schroeder tells me the mosquitoes will be worse next week because of the mix of intense heat and heavy rain. I am equally relieved and bummed out. Today, I did not apply insect repellant on purpose. Some further attempt at reconnecting to this land, or at the very least suffering toward some greater meaning, maybe?

Schroeder, a burly guy with closely shaven hair, immediately chucks a branch from the path while telling me it's not usually this bad but that the recent storm knocked down a lot of tree limbs. He has been a land manager with the Ohio Department of Natural Resources for over fifteen years and knows these woods better than anyone. His khaki cargo pants are worn down and faded from endless days out here, and he drives a forest service pickup truck just as weathered as his uniform. He is quiet and thoughtful in his responses and doesn't act like he's in much of a hurry, despite the fact that he has to coach his kid's softball game in an hour.

Regardless of mosquitoes, I am so excited by these dark wetlands that my voice is running about twice its normal speed. "Is this what the Great Black Swamp was like back in the 1800s?" I say, tossing a fallen stick into a standing pool of muck.

"I think we have a plaque up that says, you know, 'One hundred acres of virgin timber.'"

I nod quickly. My toes ball up into a fist.

Bingo.

I repeat myself, telling Ryan that's why I came here, wondering if maybe he didn't hear me the first time.

"Which is probably not *quite* accurate."

"What?" I feel a slight pang.

"It's true that it was never clear cut. But they chopped trees down, they just didn't cut everything down." This is what makes Goll Woods peculiar. The Black Swamp was absolutely razed around 1900, about the time Teddy Roosevelt was elected and James Murray

Spangler invented the vacuum cleaner across the state in Canton. Goll remained untouched until 1916, when many of the oldest, thickest trees were felled in support of the US Army during a World War I lumber shortage. "So, there are still oak trees here over four hundred years old in a forest setting, which is unheard of, really, anywhere in the state."

My spirits bounce back slightly, thinking this might be sorta, kinda like what my great-great-great-grandfather saw when he settled nearby. But still, Ryan hints that there's nothing left of the true, original Great Black Swamp. It has gone extinct like so many plants and animals around the region.

Ryan spots movement on one of the puddles and gets excited, which is something I haven't seen from his patient, calm demeanor yet. I ask what got his attention, and he says he was curious whether that was a salamander skittering around.

It strikes me that everyone is really interested in salamanders, but I don't question why. Maybe I'm worried I'll sound dumb, or maybe I'm just eager to continue talking about people we both know from my hometown. "I went to college with some crazy guys from Deshler," he says. "You probably don't know them, though."

Turns out Ryan and I are the same age. Several guys I graduated high school with ended up being his Ohio State University drinking buddies. The shared connection brings me back to my teenage years, when I'd grown into something pretty peculiar around here. I'd always done things a little differently, thanks to that carefree, isolated childhood.

By age ten, when everyone wanted to be a firefighter or a policeman, I wanted to be an archaeologist like Indiana Jones. That was until I learned you aren't issued a bullwhip and a pistol upon completing your PhD program. Coincidentally, this was the same year Laura Peterson wrote in my yearbook, "To a real weirdo."

By age twelve, when everyone wanted to be an NBA or NFL pro, I wanted to be a pyrotechnician. My dad and I both shared a love of secretly hauling back illegal fireworks from Indiana and Tennessee every summer. I spent most every July and August lighting Black Cats and Whistling Moon Travelers in isolation at the house. I got so obsessed I would meticulously mark down the order in which we should light off our family's modest Fourth of July display, because I was going to be a professional fireworks man when I grew up. That was until Mom encouragingly mentioned that I would need to be an expert in chemistry and math for that job, two subjects I was abysmal at.

By fourteen, a lot of people were beginning to make practical plans like wanting to be a dentist or UPS driver after graduation. This was also the height of grunge and alternative music, and I knew I wanted to be a rock musician. Best I could tell, there were no educational prerequisites. Plus, my odds of punching a Nazi and/or dealing with pyrotechnics on a daily basis remained surprisingly high as a professional rocker.

This fascination came courtesy of a small moment one year earlier, when I bought a book. This would prove to be the moment that I broke completely with what most folks considered normal.

It's 1993, and I have been wearing glasses, thin wire-rimmed things that need to be strapped into Croakies for gym and basketball practice, for about two years and hate them. My grades are almost entirely Cs and Ds. Everyone seems to have a girlfriend but me.

I am a depressed, alienated, greasy-faced thirteen-year-old when Mom takes me and a friend to see *Addams Family Values*. Entering the Findlay Village Mall means getting hit with a strong doughy whiff of Hot Sam Pretzels. It's just after Thanksgiving, and Christmas music tinkles just above the volume of everyone's voices. The early evening crowd passes by, mostly a flood of small children dressed in corduroy and lace with bowties and patent leather shoes, waiting turns on Santa's lap.

My friend Steve and I are killing time at B. Dalton Booksellers before the movie starts, browsing through the art section, hoping to find a book with naked women inside. The holy grail is Madonna's racy photo book *Sex*.

We don't find a single nipple in the entire store, which leads me to the adjacent music section, where I discover total snores like *The Duke Ellington Reader* and *Judy Garland: The Secret Life of an American Legend*. But the endcap grips my attention. It displays a book called *Come as You Are: The Story of Nirvana*. Nirvana is my favorite band. I own a couple of their tapes but have never seen any of the band's videos on MTV, since we live too far out in the country to get cable. The only visual evidence I have of the band is from the occasional *Rolling Stone* article in the library and the recent episode of *Saturday Night Live* I taped, where I fast forward through all the awkward skits featuring host Charles Barkley in order to watch and rewatch and rewatch both songs the band played from *In Utero*.

Steve keeps hunting for nudity, but I am gone, quickly flipping through all 344 pages of *Come as You Are*. I'm intrigued to find this is not one of those books that is dense with text. Chapters are broken up with hip, Gen X typography and lots of photos. Thrilling pictures of Cobain thrashing around onstage. Incredible images of the wreckage after the band smashed its instruments. Crude DIY concert posters. Scans of lyrics in awful, sloppy handwriting. Just like mine!

The back of the book seals the deal. In random upper and lowercase, like a ransom note, it reads: "tHe Uncensored HisTorY OF oNe of ThE World'S gREaTest RoCk bAnds."

Uncensored? I think. *Who needs nudity when you've got this?*

After some haggling, I convince Mom to buy me the book, despite the fact that the only book I've ever finished up to that point is Michael Crichton's *Jurassic Park*. Thirty-five years later, I won't be able to recall one single word or scene from *Addams Family Values*, but whole paragraphs of *Come as You Are* have become woven into my DNA.

A lot of other rock books would begin with a triumphant gig in London or Madison Square Garden. Mötley Crüe or Guns N' Roses would be described in their shirtless, chiseled glory, stage littered with panties, retreating backstage to a pile of cocaine and nudity. But *Come as You Are* opens with the band playing a benefit concert for Bosnian rape victims in an old ice hockey stadium called the Cow Palace. The star of the show is not shirtless or in leather pants but wearing an inside-out Captain America T-shirt, "decomposing blue jeans," and freshly dyed hair. This causes me to open up the set of *Encyclopedia Britannicas* on a shelf below our TV to look up words I don't totally understand, like *Bosnia*.

Deep below that blond bowl cut, my normal Northwest Ohio brain warps slightly.

In fact, everything I need to know is offered in the first few pages. It calls into question the ethics of mainstream music I'd previously enjoyed because I wanted to be part of the group of classmates who idolized GNR, Michael Jackson, and C+C Music Factory. The book points a finger at the toxic personalities of Sting and Don Henley for their posturing, bandwagon-jumping, and self-righteousness, but Azerrad might as well be talking about the friends at school. I've fallen into a dark pattern where my friends tease and hurt me, and I do anything I can to win them back. Recently, a few of them tossed me in a dumpster after lunch, after which I couldn't wait to find a way back into their circle. It was, after all, my fault for being weird.

"Kurt Cobain's reaction to bad times was as direct as can be," Azerrad writes. "And a hell of a lot more honest. He screamed." I lean closer, reread that line several times, and feel something like permission open up in my chest.

I take another trip to the family encyclopedia shelf upon coming across the line: "The band has expressed strong feelings about feminism, racism, censorship, and especially homophobia." The only one of those four words that I've heard before is *racism*. The mind beneath that bowl cut grows another couple wrinkles.

According to Azerrad, the band believed in a "do-it-yourself, be-yourself, low-tech ethos." They still shopped at thrift stores, and Cobain kept the band's MTV Video Award atop the toilet. And then the bomb: "Kurt Cobain and Krist Novoselic come from the isolated coastal logging town of Aberdeen, Washington." It's a small town that sounds a whole lot like where I live.

For the first time in my life, I am with my people.

Prior to *Come as You Are*, I was sure punk rockers were the bad guys on *Miami Vice* or the bullies in *Head of the Class*. A month later, when I close page 344, I see that being punk isn't criminal, it's a positive lifestyle choice. Punk is a loose set of guidelines that means doing things yourself, not being phony, accepting everyone for who they are—unless they are assholes. The book talks about aggressive, sweaty, middle-finger-flipping hardcore like Black Flag with the same reverence as clean-cut bands like the Beat Happening, who once released an album cover featuring a crudely sketched kitty cat sitting in a rocket. Yes, aggression is punk, but so is being kooky and being smart. Being open-minded and egalitarian is punk. Being weird is very punk. In my 1993 Northwest Ohio world, this is transgressive and eye-opening to discover. It's an unthinkable way of life for small-town guys like me.

Cobain's philosophy, which he openly cribs from '80s underground artists and labels like K Records, says that anyone can do this stuff, and you don't need any special skills to be creative. No skills necessary? This, again, speaks to me. I am in love with the idea that Cobain was inspired by the idea that just trying to express yourself is an artistic act.

The urge to be creative, and weird, and abnormal begins to burn inside me.

But, like with the swamp before me, some people will try very hard to eliminate abnormalities.

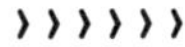

I snap back just as we near the end of Goll Woods' looping trails, still tossing branches from the path. I ask Ryan to tell those guys hello for me. I have fond memories of his buddies. They were not the ones that made my life hell later in my teens.

Next, I ask Ryan the same question I asked Melanie. Is this how dark it was in the Great Black Swamp?

"Some people said there'd be pockets of snow well into May," Ryan says. "Some said you could look behind a big tree that never got any sun, and snow would still be there. That's how dark it was."

Birds and bugs chitter all around us. A truck's loud muffler cuts through the peace, and I know we must be near the parking lot and the end of my tour.

"You see this dead ash tree right here? The emerald ash borer killed all the ash trees. Dutch elm disease killed all the elms," Ryan says. "Everything's changed from back then."

16

AN ALL-OUT WAR ON THE TREES

Tripadvisor really struggles to recommend much about Deshler. The best attraction it comes up with is Crossroads Park, a small patch of grass with a picnic table right behind Main Street where both rail lines crisscross. It frequently attracts a handful of train buffs, usually to take photos and leave town. Yelp has an even harder time; for dining it recommends one restaurant in town and another nearly thirty minutes away. Deshler hasn't had a hotel since long before I was born.

It makes me wonder: Is there any other place on Earth that offers almost nothing to outsiders? It's not just my hometown; this situation is pretty much the norm in Northwest Ohio. There are few, if any, historical points of interest aside from a handful of iron placards for long forgotten battles and, maybe, if we're being generous, Rutherford B. Hayes's home on the easternmost fringe of the old Black Swamp. There are no museums, other than the occasional county historical type. There's not even a town offering a biggest-ball-of-twine-type roadside wonder.

If anything, this place is unique for its absolute lack of uniqueness. The older I get, though, the more I appreciate that absence. Leaving Goll Woods, I realize that there are no other places I can think of that feature nothing but yardstick-straight roads and panoramic blue sky and silence. I enjoy sitting on my parents' porch and hearing nothing. Maybe that should be the draw: "Northwest Ohio: Relax, we've got nothing!"

Ohio Magazine's John Fleischman once wrote a cheeky article that read, "The Great Black Swamp is no more and this area needs a new name. Call it the Great Flatness."

During high school, when I was heartbroken or friendless, I'd crawl out my bedroom window and lie on the garage roof's gritty black shingles and stare up at the night sky. No car engines. No voices. No birds, and often no insects. Just bigness and peace and a breeze whispering through the leaves. If it was a calm night, there was absolutely no sound at all. Just gentle, welcoming silence and stars. Being so far away from a major city, the stars were prominently visible. Deshler was so isolated that you could see the faint purple glow of Toledo on the horizon to the north, just barely.

Around this time, I bought a guitar and started writing punk rock songs alone in my room. It didn't feel safe to express myself to others, and that insecurity only got worse as high school continued. If my isolated childhood was carefree and happy, my teen years were about to become far more complicated because, while I often desired being a part of a group, the second I got into a group I usually wanted out. I wanted to be a free-spirited punk but also normal and popular.

No matter how hard I tried, I could never be normal enough, and that often made life miserable. Sometime between my sophomore and senior years, when I'd read *Come as You Are* for the third or fourth time, a strange thing happened: I was simultaneously the leading tackler on the football team and also the target of bullying. The rumor I was gay started at school, and it felt like everyone stopped talking to me. I did have a few core friends who stuck with me, like my buddy Terry, but in a school so small it felt like the entire world had suddenly turned its back. The main group who started harassing me was a group of guys I thought were my closest friends. They completely ignored me, or when they did say something in the hallway, it usually involved some homophobic slur. My first response was to lash out, to yell, to deny. But this, of course just made the taunting multiply. Sometimes our cordless home phone would ring late at night and the other end of the line would be filled with giggling boys followed by a snippet of the rap-rock band Korn's "Faget" (a real work of 1990s poetic genius featuring that offensive title screamed repeatedly). Some nights they would mix it up and the phone line would fill with orgasm moans from a porno. For a long while after that, my shoulders got tense whenever the phone rang.

Eventually, I pretended like this treatment didn't bother me. I shrugged and smiled and acted like this was normal. This left me spending hours driving around Deshler alone on the weekends, just so I wouldn't have to sit at my house by myself feeling like a complete failure. I'd listen to WIOT or my Sonic Youth and Jesus Lizard and Breeders CDs. Sometimes those kids I wanted to be friends with so badly would yell obscenities at me from the parking lots they hung out in. Sometimes if I got brave—or saw that there were some less aggressive folks hanging around too—I'd get out, but always with the anxiety that nobody liked me and that things could get ugly in a hurry around here if I wasn't on my toes. When I'd get home, I'd crawl atop the garage and look at the sky.

In hindsight, I see how much harder and scarier it is to actually be queer in a small town or anywhere with narrow views on sex and gender and know that was not the torment I went through. I see now how privileged and lucky I was. But at the time, it felt like I was hanging from a lonely branch over a deep pit, and my grip was slipping.

Some of the few comforts at this time were chapters in *Come as You Are* about Cobain's childhood. Yes, he was the coolest art weirdo in the world and started his life in a rural town, which was great. But I really leaned on Cobain's stories of alienation and being bullied and of being called queer, too. "Small town mentality," Mudhoney bassist and Cobain's childhood friend Matt Lukin said in the book. "Narrow-minded people who looked at something they weren't used to as something bad."

"In a small town," Shelli Novoselic, ex-wife of Nirvana bassist Krist, told Azerrad, "you're different and you're the freak."

I'd found my people in this book, but that didn't mean I wasn't drawn back to those toxic friendships. It didn't mean I wasn't willing to do anything to gain back the approval of the people so focused on hurting me.

After several months, the taunting went away only when I buried those feelings. I learned to stop expressing myself in any way, shape, or form. This allowed me to seem like just enough of an outgoing, macho dude that I was accepted as normal. I finally understood that you should never act too proud or happy, but also don't be too sullen or sensitive. The perfect Northwest Ohioan, it seemed, was even keeled and unable to harness any emotional range.

The exception, of course, was when you were pointing out others' shortcomings. It was a weird, dysfunctional way to live, and unfortunately, I sometimes teased other kids and partook in embarrassing them, all in a sad attempt at keeping my own social standing. I felt very guilty for acting that way.

But I was never able to detach completely. I became a person who lived their life in the darkness. I was the three-year football letterman who took a date to the prom but also the weirdo who went by himself to the record store in Bowling Green to look for strange music that made me feel less alone in the world. I'd rent movies about alienated oddballs, like Richard Linklater's *SubUrbia* and Kevin Smith's *Clerks*, and watch them alone. I read books in study hall instead of flirting with girls like the other guys; a recent favorite was *On the Road*, probably because it was about a guy who didn't fit in at home, so he went wandering around, often by himself. I wrote songs for my imaginary grunge band, The Losers, often about girls I was secretly in love with.

I felt ashamed to be this way.

It all reminds me of a curious scene toward the end of *The Story of the Great Black Swamp*. Out of absolutely nowhere, the camera focuses on a single-engine propeller plane landing on a rain-slicked runway, and our host, Glenn, steps out of the cabin. My first reaction was, *Did Glenn fly here? Or, wait, is Glenn just pretending to fly? And if so, why?* Because flight has had absolutely nothing to do with this story so far.

"Farmers in Northwest Ohio find a beauty in all this flatness. Some confess to bewilderment as to why anyone would ever want to farm on the side of a hill. Or to not be able to see the end of a row a mile down the end of a field." Glenn peers directly into the camera, and it's like he is staring across the years, right at me, like he knows the torment I went through in my teens, like he has a boom box with Korn queued up. "They love straightness."

Straightness, normalcy, no drama. This is a place with no patience for roadside attractions or '90s high schoolers secretly trying to live punk rock lifestyles. The more I keep digging, the more I wonder if this love of straightness and normalcy isn't just my experience but a deeper need. A need that stems from the herculean task of civilizing the Great Black Swamp. Because the strength and vision needed for that job couldn't simply be accomplished on a whim.

After the Buckeye Traction Ditcher tore up Northwest Ohio in the 1890s, towns like Deshler quickly began sprouting up across the region. None of them have a very exciting birthing story. "Nothing to see here," they seemed to say. But in almost every case, there were struggles, and growing pains, wildness, lawlessness, and dreaming. It's just that we are too modest to do our dreaming in public, especially when there is work to be done. Massive amounts of work.

"One thing became clear from the start," Glenn says. "That any farming done here would have to be done on a heroic scale comparable to the heroic task it took to clear the swamp....They fought a valiant battle against the swamp and the swamp left its toll on them—weathered, valiant, rough-hewn, unvarnished people. *But they won*," Glenn states, still quizzically standing beside that single-engine propeller plane. "The Great Black Swamp is no more."

Master thespian that he is, Glenn adds another curveball: "Or is it? When it rains in Northwest Ohio, the old swamp returns. More of a lake than a swamp."

The film runs scratchy footage of flooded streets and yards turned to shallow pools of standing dark water—not unlike what I saw in the ditches around Deshler and in the streets of Carey. The documentary cuts to airborne images of waterlogged fields stretching for miles; we see mud-colored water all the way to the horizon. We are not told whether Glenn is piloting the plane from which these shots are taken, but I have my doubts.

To be clear, this is not catastrophic flooding. Nobody is losing their home or business or life because of these floods. It's usually only a few inches deep, but this flooding is a sign that our drainage tiles and ditches and rivers can only whisk away so much water. That hard clay soil naturally guards the surface like a million acres of Saran Wrap. When the area hangs on to that standing water for a few days, it's not hard to imagine that this is what it must have been like every day when the area was first settled.

Here, almost at the end of the film, and at its most nonsensical point thanks to all the airplane stuff, *The Story of the Great Black Swamp* surprises me by finally starting to reveal a deeper meaning. Here, in the closing moments of the documentary, Glenn harnesses all the light and darkness of the area, the same duality he'd display in *The Dark Half*.

Remember the spooky synth score, that horror movie music? Remember the tractor footage burying us alive? Remember detail after detail after detail about how the Great Black Swamp was a geographical misery machine, all delivered by the sweetest old man you ever met? Remember? I'm struck by the realization that *The Story of the Great Black Swamp* was never a celebration of America's can-do spirit or Ohio's agricultural prowess. No, this has been a sixty-minute condemnation of the way we abuse our ecological gifts. This has been an alarm bell disguised as a history lesson.

"They had no idea the place would be so miserable and that the trees would be so tall, and so wide across that one or two persons couldn't possibly fell them. It would take a massive attack to clear the forest, and all-out commitment to eliminate the trees," Glenn says, like a football coach brimming with quiet intensity.

This guy, can we please award him a posthumous Oscar?

Newcomers to Northwest Ohio were tired, frustrated, and sick. When not shaking uncontrollably from ague (the local term for malaria), shitting themselves to death from cholera, or fighting back predatory forest monsters, these new Ohioans were dreaming up ways to settle down and get normal.

And yet, normal was just on the horizon. James B. Hill's invention had actually morphed this place into the Garden of Ohio pretty quickly. The story of the region's deforestation has to be one of America's fastest land-flipping jobs, which is saying something. In my research, I'm hard-pressed to find any wilderness that was modified into habitable space on such a scale and with such speed.

By New Year's Day 1900, Deshler's population had quadrupled to about 1,600 and finally felt like the boomtown it had set out to become. Quick money was rolling in as the timber was sold in absurd quantities. Farms and homes began springing up in the cleared land's wake.

The radical change to the landscape must have been shocking. Glenn calls it "an all-out war on the trees." The sound of moaning tree limbs and wild animals was replaced by the sound of lumberjacks, known as specialists, who began ripping across

Northwest Ohio, sending the most valuable logs to Canada and Europe for shipbuilding. Timber boomtowns like Deshler sprang up to capitalize on the leftover lumber, crafting barrel staves, cigar boxes, handles, and wheel spokes. Anything that couldn't be turned into profit was destroyed. Burning bees became popular, in which men would rapidly cut down entire forests that had stood for hundreds of years, let the dead trees dry out for a season, and then set those woods on fire. The ashes were often collected and sold to soap manufacturers.

In a few years, the Great Black Swamp had been violently converted from a pristinely dense wetland to a million acres of bone-dry farm fields. Settlers often completed this transition by hiring a dynamiter to blow any remaining stumps out of the ground, reportedly rocketing them as high as 150 feet in the air. This was the exact moment the flat, infinite Northwest Ohio landscape was truly created. In retrospect, it was also the moment we seemingly threw away any meaningful recollection of the abnormalities that made the Great Black Swamp unique. We forgot that this land was here long before us and is much tougher than we are.

Our collective love of straightness was about to begin.

The swamp's destruction was celebrated as progress. It was our right to do as we saw fit, and here we were, turning this uninhabitable land into something normal. Virtually no one publicly took issue with this plan, save for Perrysburg doctor Dwight R. Canfield. "Is man like an insect that passes over and attacks our fruit trees and destroys them? What is man but another animal?" he wrote, reflecting on the Black Swamp's conversion later in life. "Will he some day and some time be destroyed off the face of the Earth that it may return to its former state as it was before the creation? Deep in the silences of the forests, I am constrained to wonder!"

This rapid growth meant Deshler, and communities like it, were often not owned by their residents. Much like Wild West boomtowns centered on silver mines or oil strikes, a majority of Northwest Ohio's towns were owned by speculators who had snapped up the land decades earlier. After John Deshler sold his holdings, my hometown was mostly owned by a Cincinnati lawyer named Florien Giauque at the beginning of the twentieth century. In addition to purchasing a large percentage of the properties on both sides of Main Street and about one hundred homes in town, the Swiss émigré also cleared and drained over two thousand acres of farmland around the area. Giauque, a sort of Renaissance man, also penned how-to books on being a notary public, being a constable, and negotiating dowries.

Deshler's numerous taverns and inns all had constructed raised boardwalks to keep boots from sloshing through the mud. These ad hoc sidewalks stretched the length of town, down beyond the unpainted plank homes with gaping doors. While Giauque's investment dragged this section of swamp toward the twentieth century, this change, like countless developments before it, came booby-trapped with consequences. In its aftermath, a rootless and rowdy society was created in about the time it took to dynamite a tree stump. Nobody owned a stake here, therefore the door was opened to all sorts of trouble. Deshler soon earned the nickname "The Wildest Town of the Four Counties."

Historian Prudence Dangler adds: "There were saloons and houses of prostitution on the town's main throughfare, which rivaled each other in doing prominent business with the transient population of the period. Men from the canal, woodsmen, teamsters, travelling men, railroaders, and farmers from the outlying frontier settlements who came in to do their marketing made up the business customers of the town." Deshler got so rough that curfews were introduced, including an 8:00 p.m. one for minors.

Soon, Deshler and most of the other romping, stomping boomtowns toned things down significantly. When the lumber was fully depleted and the oil was drained from the ground (for a flicker of time the area was also home to a minor oil boom; nearby Findlay sat atop a huge reserve and is still headquarters of Marathon Oil), the swashbuckling lumberjacks and wildcatters vanished, and the land was inherited almost exclusively by farmers. The early-to-bed-early-to-rise set swarmed to the area and gladly transformed this Midwestern Deadwood into dead weight. Just as quickly as the unforgiving swamp was converted into a wild boomtown, it then transformed into a conservative, quiet, friendly place where European immigrants forged a solid, if unfussy, life.

Forgettable, unassuming Northwest Ohio had become a microcosm of the American Dream. The goal here was never to get wealthy beyond belief but for people of modest means to own their future and provide for their family. The goal was to be in charge of your own destiny for the first time, away from the societal restrictions of the East and South. This was freedom.

But this idyllic success wouldn't last. In a matter of decades, simply owning forty acres and feeding your family with that toil would not be enough.

17
CORN CITY

This afternoon, I am sitting somewhere very familiar: Deshler's Edwin Wood Memorial Library. This small, one-room brick building was among my favorite places as a kid. Once Mom started working here, I was often stuck waiting around after school for her shift to end, reading Shel Silverstein or a Guinness World Records book or the *Haunted Ohio* series, or just wandering the stacks, plucking books at random to see what was inside. While I often complained that I was bored, I secretly loved it. I would wander blindly from romance novels to histories of flight, poetry, cookbooks, and *How to Build a Robot* by Steve Lindblom, which always fascinated me.

Today, everything in the library feels a lot different than back then. Mom retired a few years ago, Deshler Elementary has been torn down next door, and the space feels more claustrophobic than I remember. Every spare inch of space is being utilized, most noticeably with hardbacks stacked on flat surfaces like a funky used book shop. One librarian tells me they have been awarded a grant for an expansion, but construction hasn't begun yet.

I settle into a spot I vaguely recall as a child. I remember wondering if the gray-haired old ladies operating the hulking lightbox screen of the microfiche station weren't playing some video game I didn't understand. It is a game, sort of. Kind of a scavenger hunt. I sit down and start scrolling through ancient editions of *The Deshler Flag*. The paper was founded in 1900, during the town's Deadwood era, but those issues of the paper aren't nearly as exciting as I'd hoped. I am hunting for eye-popping yellow journalism about barroom brawls, muddied faces, maybe mysterious wagons selling miracle tonics. Instead, the newspaper's editorial staff was already more focused on that transition into being a hardworking, low-drama place to call home.

I continue scrolling forward through the years, black and white images blurring by like a high-speed train. Every time I stop there always seems to be at least one article about a recent automobile injury or death, often alongside church bake sales and high school science fairs. I am reminded that I once conducted an experiment where I tried to prove that playing Nirvana's *Incesticide* album repeatedly would help a plant grow faster. Results were inconclusive, and as I remember, so was my grade. Every one of the *Flag*'s front pages for years also features a sidebar called "Corn City Kernels," where the editor gives out folksy bits of first-person town news, including one that mentioned with great enthusiasm the sighting of two deer, which apparently had become extinct in these parts after the swamp was drained and the timber felled.

Sometime during the early half of the 1900s, the town had earned the nickname the Corn City, which is appropriate, but also odd, since we are far from being a city. If they are counting individual stalks of corn as citizens, we must rival Mumbai and Mexico City for population. Along the way, we picked up a second nickname, too: the Crossroads of the B&O, but I prefer the corn one.

The microfiche machine keeps history whizzing by. The blur stops on a June 1949 issue, and it's pretty much the usual bake sales and auto wreck news, except squeezed near the top left corner is a modest headline: "Deshler Story." Below, it reads: "The feature story on Deshler is scheduled to run in the *New York Times* this Sunday."

It must be a joke or a typo. It might make sense to see my town appear in the *Toledo Blade* or *Tractor Aficionado Magazine*, but the most famous newspaper on the planet? I carefully drag the microfiche forward a week and discover a longer article discussing residents' mixed reactions to being featured in a *New York Times* article, apparently written by a reporter named David Dempsey.

Nowhere does it mention *what* this article was about. It just takes for granted that everyone in town has read it already. What could have been so noteworthy here? Maybe a secret buried beneath the town? A murder, a cult, Dillinger's treasure? Maybe we did, in fact, attempt some wacky publicity stunt, like that town in Texas that renamed itself after the Dish Network in 2005.

What would have been the 1949 equivalent? Asbestos Heights?

"Have you guys ever heard about a *New York Times* article written about Deshler back in 1949?" I ask my parents when I get back to their house.

"Nope," Dad says, watching NASCAR time trials on TV.

"*Here?*" Mom says, playing a board game with my son. She sounds sort of surprised but also not really all that impressed.

I open my computer and discover with only a few keystrokes that, yes, there was an article written about my hometown in the freaking

New York Times! I excitedly yell something to my mom, and she responds by asking if ham is OK for dinner.

This article is not just some blurb about a train derailment or our stalks of corn finally being granted citizenship. It's a *huge* feature spread across five pages titled "Picture of a Small Town in the Atomic Age." It was published on June 5, 1949, and starts off white-hot, claiming Deshler would like to see the world made over in its "own less truculent image," implying that the United Nations could learn a few things from my hometown.

Why didn't anyone ever tell me about this story? Anywhere outside of Northwest Ohio, they'd put up a gleaming brass David Dempsey plaque outside of town hall or feature some mention of this article on their welcome signage. More importantly, why did *The New York Times* pick Deshler at all? One *Flag* editorial speculated that the *Times* chose our town because it was the smallest place Harry Truman made a speech during his presidential campaign the year before. It's possible, but Dempsey's article doesn't explicitly say so, though he does mention the future president's brief stopover.

In 1948, Truman was in a furious three-way race for the White House between himself, Thomas Dewey, and Strom Thurmond. Harry Truman famously used whistle-stop tours as a staple of spreading his message. According to the National Railroad Hall of Fame, "He traveled 31,000 miles and made 352 speeches, many of them to voters in cities and towns most Americans had never heard of," all from a custom rail car named *Ferdinand Magellan*. Henry County voted for Dewey, and it was speculated that perhaps the *Times* was checking in to see how this conservative enclave of the country was fairing under Truman, a Democrat. But still, *Why Deshler*? Judging by the story he submitted, I'm not certain David Dempsey even knew. It's almost like he tossed a dart at a map, or maybe his car broke down here, since he really gives no qualifiers for why this article's wholesome Midwestern setting should be a lesson to the world. "Deshler wonders why the UN can't solve some of its problems after the fashion of the town council," he claims.

While it feels pretty flimsy to think that Deshler was demanding the planet's governing bodies act more like us and calls into question a lot about this article, there's no denying that this story is a perfect time capsule of post-swamp life in Northwest Ohio. A world pretty much exactly like those visionaries dreamed of: The Garden of Ohio and a solid place to raise a family. Dempsey has a great eye for those mellow, midcentury scenes. "Young men who fought their way over battlefields a few years ago are plowing stubblefields now," he notes. At this time, my grandfather Don had just returned from Utah Beach with a Purple Heart, and he and grandmother Norma opened a tractor sales and repair shop on Main Street. My Aunt Marianne was a toddler, and my father was still three years from being born. They aren't mentioned in the story, sadly.

Almost by accident, this article seems to operate as a snapshot of how the twentieth century was the former Great Black Swamp's time to rise. A peaceful stretch when hearty crops grew like grass and agricultural incomes rose. The money was so good that, according to Dempsey, "farmers were installing radios on their tractors and taking their vacations in Florida."

Dempsey was a well-respected writer. Aside from being a *Times* reporter, the Illinois native (yep, I checked to see if maybe he was from Deshler or nearby—no luck) was a celebrated war correspondent and literary critic. He penned several nonfiction books and a novel. His one-act play, *It Ain't Brooklyn*, won a contest in 1944 judged by, among others, Pulitzer-winning Broadway legend Moss Hart. So, it's a real treat to see Dempsey dissect the town's inner workings, even if the bigger picture doesn't totally add up.

This portrait of the area is a striking contrast to the grim reports of 1800s. *Times* readers were given a glimpse of what would eventually become that prevailing view of this corner of the Midwest, especially if you ask Bill Bryson or my old friends from college who called me the Hillbilly. "Excitement? There isn't much," he writes.

> Deshler goes to bed early and gets up at daybreak. It is a law-abiding town, too. Most of the 102 cases on the Mayor's docket for the last three years were for traffic violations, although a few offenders were charged, somewhat quaintly, with "noise and clamor in the night season."
>
> For whatever the physical image of the town may be, there is a pattern underneath it by which the community conducts the real business of living. Perhaps nowhere in the United States will you hear a more spirited defense of "the American way of life," which means pretty much life as it is lived in Deshler—democratic, egalitarian, easy going, and decently wholesome, if a little dull.

Dempsy points out that there are no mansions in Deshler and adds a town councilman's claim: "The only bottle of champagne ever seen around here was used to christen the new standby engine in the power plant." However, the article notes that there are also no slums seen and "not much attention is paid to 'prettifying' the town," which he compares to some Sinclair Lewis novels. "'We don't need chrome trimmings and smart storefronts,' a merchant told me. 'People around here judge us by what's inside.'"

But, in true Northwest Ohio fashion, there's something dark and insecure beneath this cheerful normalcy. While the article never mentions the Great Black Swamp, Dempsey does cryptically refer to the town's foundation as a cash grab for speculators like Florien Giauque and John Deshler. "Until four years ago most of the business district and half of the houses were owned by an estate in Cincinnati." Giauque died in 1921, but it's safe to assume that's the estate in question. "Businessmen raised $150,000 and Deshler literally 'bought itself back.' Houses and stores were resold to their occupants, and within six months some $30,000 in improvements and repairs had been made."

Yet another story nobody ever mentioned but maybe should have been celebrating with pride. The town collectively raised roughly $2.5 million in today's money and took their small town back from some greedy land baron? This should be a movie or a Broadway musical. Someone call Moss Hart! Instead, it has gone unmentioned. I'm sure if you asked one of the old-timers of my youth, they would have just yawned and said something like, "Oh, everybody has to buy their town back from Swiss émigré/land speculator/author of a how-to manual on negotiating dowries at some time or another. It was just our turn."

Dempsey's story is a curious artifact. It never finds its focus and simply meanders for most of its length, detailing that it takes only ten minutes to walk across town and calling the grain elevator a "prairie skyscraper." He quotes the mayor and some farmers and the *Deshler Flag*'s publisher, and it all just oozes Midwestern modesty. But these scenes are interwoven with a pretty sweaty attempt to link everything to global politics, continuing to urge the world to operate more like a Midwestern village.

Near the end, Dempsey focuses on the way our small town soberly dealt with the changes brought on by a recent financial recession, in particular how grain prices had dropped and families suddenly saw less money than they had since the war.

"The women bought nothing but ready-to-wear dresses a few years back," the manager of the town's department store says. "Now they're buying yard goods again and making their own clothes. That's a sign we're getting back to normal."

Dempsey counters by noting, "A lot of people in town are not sure how far back to 'normal' Deshler can go without getting into trouble."

That line sticks with me, as I'm lying in bed at my parents' house, hearing a nearby train whistle cut through the darkness and stars. While Dempsey's mention of "normal" is talking, specifically, about the financial norms of these farm families making do with less, it strikes me that he could just as easily be talking about all the other ways this place strives to maintain the status quo.

"If an economic twister should hit," the article notes,

> Deshler will be about as well prepared for it as one town can get. It is unlikely that anyone will be evicted from his home, or that the bank will foreclose on loans. (It did not, for example, during all the

> depression.) The power plant won't turn off the light of unemployed who cannot meet their bills. Stores will do more business on credit, grocers will trade flour for fresh eggs and vegetables. A lot of "necessities" will be dispensed with—cars and telephones, for instance. If the worst comes, Deshler will dig in and live on faith.

In other words, nobody has ever been more prepared to shrug, and smile, and go back to normal. And that's just what we did, right about the time Deshler—and all of Northwest Ohio—should have been paying a lot more attention to what was going on below the surface of our soil.

18

CROP ECONOMICS FOR OHIO

A few nights after returning from Deshler, I am electrified by corn. All I can think about is corn, like some sleuth with a murder board zigzagged in red string connecting suspects, with an enormous question mark at the center, still missing one crucial piece of evidence to tie it all together. That's because, tonight, I think I have solved the 2014 algae crisis. And, yes, it has to do with the Great Black Swamp and towns like Deshler, but primarily it deals with our old frenemy: corn. Animal feed, tortillas, sweet corn, Orville Redenbacher.

It's way past midnight when I make this discovery. The only sound in the house is the rattle of the air conditioner vents. My son is sleeping upstairs, and I should also be asleep, but I am focused, deeply focused, on the thrillingly titled 1962 brochure *Crop Economics for Ohio*. This twenty-page booklet is some kind of mix between a scientific study and a hard sales push funded by the USDA and Ohio State University. On the surface it is kitschy, harmless, and kind of ridiculous. I mean, a cartoon ear of corn serves as a mascot for the entire endeavor, but look deeper and that cartoon proves to be a sort of unwitting Tony the Tiger of ecological collapse. I suspect this cartoon is the key to get from an untouched Black Swamp to Dempsey's *New York Times* example of small-town perfection to the prime suspect in 2014's toxic algae epidemic.

The corncob mascot is hand-drawn, blending the scrappiness of a political cartoon and the carefree advertising style of the era. Its first appearance shows this human-sized ear of corn holding a giant wooden mallet with its own husks (serving as arms), slamming down on a carnival strongman game. The corn looks on, determined, while the ringer zips up the board and clangs a bell labeled "CROP PROFITS." Tiny dollar signs burst from the bell like a fireworks display. A caption reads: "To make a satisfactory income from crops alone, a farmer will have to operate a fairly large farm to obtain the necessary volume of business."

While Lake Erie's water turning to neon green toxic slime is more complicated than a goofy comic book corncob, it's closer to the answer than you'd think. That's because the ear of corn is here to ferry us through the complex subject matter of the brochure with silliness and joy. It implies that farmers of the era, too, were not encouraged to think about the environment with any seriousness. While the pitfalls of bigger-is-better, capitalism-to-the-max thinking are obvious today, sixty years ago it was such a new idea that sales brochures like this had to be printed in order to inform people. More than likely, if you saw that respected institutions like the USDA and Ohio State were encouraging this trend, you probably figured it must be sound advice. There was trust in our institutions at that time.

How many small family farmers saw this simple brochure and bought into its promise of wealth? How many of the self-sustaining farmers from Dempsey's 1949 article decided that they could avoid going back to "normal" by wringing out every inch of their modest land in favor of productivity?

The main takeaway from this carnival strongman section urges farmers to focus solely on corn instead of diversifying their output, because that farmer could earn twice as much money as the old way of juggling livestock, wheat, soybeans, and tomatoes. On page after page, the cartoon ear of corn pops back in to make monoculture farming look as playful and easy as an episode of 1962's number-one TV show, *The Beverly Hillbillies*. One image features the corn snipping a bill labeled "CROP COSTS" in half, and another shows it joyfully sliding down a bar graph representing the steep decline of costs per bushel for crop yields.

Northwest Ohio has a long relationship with corn. Even before the land's settlement, it was as if the region were custom built to raise nothing but tall, green stalks of it. In 1794, General "Mad" Anthony Wayne slaughtered the Northwest Indian Confederation, comprising the Ottawa, Seneca, Miami, and other tribes, in the Battle of Fallen Timbers near modern-day Toledo and noted, in a report to Congress, that along the outskirts of the Great Black Swamp he had never "beheld such immense fields of corn, in any part of America, from Canada to Florida." Upon seeing this agricultural wonder of Native effort, he ordered the fields burned to the ground.

By the time the Buckeye Traction Ditcher had drained the land and lumberjacks had clearcut the trees and blasted the stumps halfway to the moon, farmers found that the swamp forest had built up a rich, black layer of rotted organic matter. Thousands of years of wetland decay left behind such fertile soil that nearly anything would grow. The area was, indeed, the Garden of Ohio and immediately made an impact on the state's agriculture production. By 1910, those newly settled Black Swamp counties led all other sections of the state in amounts of feedable crops sold. By 1930, the former Black Swamp was the most completely farmed area in the state.

It must have been hard to believe that only a generation earlier, settlers were fighting malaria, wolves, and six feet of mud. Now, those same people could provide for a family and control their own destiny.

I am reminded of my great-great-great-grandfather Henry Wensink. In 1896, the *Northwest Signal* noted that he filed a petition for a permit to dig a ditch for his 159 acres outside of Deshler in Section 13 of Bartlow Township. There is no record of whether he used a Buckeye Traction Ditcher for the job, but chances are high, considering this was about the same time James B. Hill was producing Ditchers just a few miles away. Hell, they may have known each other. Section 13 is just down the road from my childhood home; I played in this ditch during the dry summer months and rode alongside it on my bike, and later my car, never knowing its history. Henry Wensink, from what I can tell, was a fairly poor Dutch immigrant who came to Northwest Ohio after venturing around the East Coast and Cleveland. I am surprisingly moved, realizing that this drainage ditch contained the dreams and hopes of my family. It represented the simple goal of honest work and freedom. Not to mention, this was a choice that eventually led to my own existence. Sure, I was picked on in high school, but those struggles feel pretty small compared to what these settlers went through. I had food on the table and loving parents and enough spare money to buy a Sonic Youth CD once in a while. That's a pretty cushy life, one in which I never once had to fend off an angry wolf sticking its face through my bedroom wall. What would Great-Great-Great-Grandpa Henry have thought to see all that prosperity stemming from this single ditch digging permit? Before tonight, I had never wondered about his dream or the dreams of thousands of other families in the Great Black Swamp. I am not the first person to seek refuge in Northwest Ohio.

Somewhere around 1:00 a.m., I try to calculate how many millions of gallons of runoff the Wensinks have sent into Lake Erie since 1896. My dad is not a farmer, but my family tree is filled with farmers. What fraction of responsibility do we hold? It quickly becomes clear I don't have the math skills for this job, so I write the Henry County Engineer's Office to see if they want to take a guess. After my request passes through several hands, presumably because nobody has ever made such an abnormal request, conservation engineer Nathan Wilhelm seems pretty engaged in this oddball challenge. After a little difficulty pinning down exactly which ditch my forefather dug, he emails: "I looked at the ditch that runs along the west side of the county line. This one goes through a farm that is Wensink owned so I figured we would try that one."

According to Wilhelm, this single ditch is 25,000 feet long (nearly 5 miles) and is fed from a watershed of about 1.87 square miles, and it takes in an average rainfall of 33 inches per year. Wilhelm's best estimate is that this lone ditch sees approximately 6.4 million gallons of water pass through it each year. He warns me that this is more of a back of the napkin calculation, and notes, "I am not stamping my PE (Professional Engineer) License on this. Haha."

That means, by my own back-of-napkin math, that Henry Wensink's small ditch has most likely sent 832 million gallons of water into Lake Erie over the last nearly 130 years. That's the equivalent of an entire reservoir, or eight hundred large swimming pools. And this is only a fraction of all the ditches in Northwest Ohio. And there were thousands of other families like mine working hard throughout the twentieth century.

The same year as the *New York Times* story, the USDA claimed, Ohio grew over 202 million bushels of corn. That year, Henry County ranked as one of the highest-producing counties in the state, averaging about 58 bushels of dried corn kernels per acre. About the weight of a female hippo.

But if Northwest Ohio's farmers wanted to follow the advice of the cartoon ear of corn, they couldn't just buy extra seeds and plant more of the same crop. To really take it to the next level, their fields would require a tune-up. At this point in the 1962 brochure, the ear of corn is wearing a rain slicker and holding an umbrella over its head during a storm, which is odd, because I always thought plants were supposed to be a big fan of rain. The ear stares down at a cartoon ditch with a pipe gushing water. "High Yields Require Well Drained Land," the text reads, going on to note that if a farmer invests a little money in updating their drainage system—which likely was made of now decayed clay pipe still leftover from the 1890s—the profits could go through the roof. Citing Northwest Ohio soil specifically, income could rise from $175 per acre to $475 per acre for every 150 pounds of fertilizer applied on drained land. It must have been hard to argue with this weirdly aquaphobic ear of corn promising that you'll make almost three times as much money if you plant only corn, drain the land, and bomb it with fertilizer. That last part—the fertilizer—was kind of offhandedly thrown into this sale pitch, but it had some of the most serious repercussions.

By the time the brochure was printed in the early 1960s, that rich swamp soil had already lost practically all of its nutrients. To make up the difference, nitrogen and phosphorus, in the form of manure and synthetic fertilizer, were added to the fields. According to another USDA report, a few years after that brochure was published, an estimated 3.5 million tons of primary plant nutrients were applied to corn acres. By 1985, plant nutrient use more than tripled to 10.6 million tons. Not surprisingly, corn acreage increased by almost 27 percent during this period.

Today, US farmers use more fertilizer on corn than on any other crop.

But our cartoon ear is not done; the next section of the brochure details how farmers could make *even more* money by using new tractors and combines to do the labor. This was the jet-set Kennedy-era America, and most likely beasts of burden were something from your father's generation. But agricultural technology was developing rapidly, and whatever machinery you were using was probably already outdated. Plus, the price was dropping significantly for farm equipment, and low-interest loans were readily available. We know that this, too, is a good thing because our ear of corn rides a tractor speeding along at a rate that would win it the Indy 500. The smokestack belches out little black dollar signs.

This profit-focused mentality that encouraged farmers to produce massive amounts of corn—which required massive amounts of fertilizer and drainage, plus the expectation that they would increase the number of acres farmed—offered them an opportunity to earn a middle-class, or even higher, income. This probably sounded like a pretty sweet deal, since that middle-class lifestyle was already becoming harder to attain for modest farmers. It was also a recipe for ecological disaster. But we didn't know that yet.

This brochure and other efforts like it seemingly changed Northwest Ohio's landscape overnight yet again. The USDA claims that in 1965 the entire state of Ohio produced only 225 million bushels of corn, which evened out to about 74 bushels per acre. That was already a 32 percent increase from just about fifteen years earlier, back when David Dempsey was bumming around Deshler. But if we assume many farmers took the brochure's advice and we go forward another fifteen years, things get intense. What was once dubbed the Garden of Ohio was, by 1980, the Kingdom of Corn. The state now produced a whopping 440 million bushels, reaping 113 bushels per acre. Henry County, bursting at the seams with so much corn it's hard to believe that it wasn't growing in my baby crib at the time, was producing 9.2 million bushels, having sharply increased its average bushels per acre to 124.

The back cover of the brochure shows the ear of corn sitting behind a desk, wearing a pair of wire-rimmed glasses and smoking a pipe, studying his ledger. Bushels are up. Profits look good. The story is over.

It's hard to wrap our minds around these numbers of acres and bushels and years, but the bottom line remains that the state's corn production rose 126 percent in a little over three decades. The same acre that produced a small zoo animal's worth of dried corn in 1949 was now cranking out the same weight as a baby blue whale by 1980.

All that fertilizer needed to go somewhere.

19

THE BEGINNING OF THE BEGINNING

Part of the reason it takes me so long to work through all twenty pages of *Crop Economics for Ohio* has nothing to do with cartoonish corn. It's because I keep looking around the kitchen, mostly staring at the cutlery set. My future ex-wife and I are trying to divvy up our assets and settle our divorce. Recently, we split up some of the knives, but I fought hard to keep the nice ones that were given to me as a Christmas gift some years back. Looking at them, I feel a strange mix of shame and pride. Proud that I stood up for myself for once and embarrassed that I picked a fight about something so unimportant.

I fought hard to hang on to my marriage, too. Though it was starting to feel like a real disaster, our family was the last group I truly felt a part of and the last group I wanted to be a member of. But I was pushed to the breaking point after feeling betrayed and confused and lost. After several painful months of letting this relationship deteriorate so I could hang onto the marriage, it finally broke.

My friend Kevin recently gave me a book called *When Things Fall Apart* by Buddhist nun Pema Chödrön. Born Deirdre Blomfield-

Brown and raised Catholic on a farm, Chödrön eventually found solace in Tibetan Buddhism after a painful divorce. Her short lessons encourage you not to fight against discomfort and pain when life feels like it is exploding before your very eyes but to acknowledge and live with those emotions. It has slowly given me a sorely needed foundation to stand on.

Recently, on the worst night of this divorce process, I collapsed on this very kitchen floor, alone, sobbing so hard I couldn't stand, crying so deeply my lungs and my throat and my back were on fire with pain, convulsing in a way that felt like I might just throw up a vital organ at any moment. The only way to soothe myself was repeating a line from Chödrön's book: "Hopelessness is just the beginning of the beginning." I said it over and over and over until I found the calmness to finally stand.

I never imagined this disaster would become my life, but does anyone? There was a time, after I graduated high school and went to college, that it seemed like she was the one person I'd always needed. We made each other better, I think. For a while, at least.

› › › › › ›

We met sophomore year of college in Dayton, Ohio, while waiting in line at the dorm post office. When we started dating, the world was edgy about whether or not all the computers would crash in a few months on New Year's Day 2000. Since high school, I'd gotten really good at hiding my quirks, and we happened to meet at the peak of my normal period. I wore khaki pants and Tommy cologne; I had a college radio show, belonged to a small fraternity, and, like everyone on campus, drank myself into oblivion each weekend. I was almost twenty, still a virgin, and had only ever kissed a few girls. The most serious relationship I'd ever had lasted for a month when I was seventeen. Whenever I was attracted to a woman, all those insecurities from high school came back. When I really liked a girl, I was terrified to even express myself enough to let her know that I liked her. Instead, I began daydreaming about how in love we could be if only she would magically notice me.

I was so insecure at the time that I had difficulty making eye contact—and still do, frankly. I had to teach myself to remember to look people in the eye when they spoke.

She was a Sun-In blonde with an outgoing personality. She had just changed her major from political science to communications and had recently quit the track team so she wouldn't have to wake up so early. The first time we hung out we sat in my dorm room and split a twelve-pack of Milwaukee's Best Light. We quickly fell in love. I didn't experience those weird anxieties like with other women because it felt like we'd known each other our whole lives. We were a perfect match: she was a misfit with a type-A personality, and I was a misfit who was happy to be a people pleaser.

She urged me to get out of my comfort zone and do unthinkable things for country boys like me, such as studying abroad in France with her. When I exposed my weirdness to the daylight, like my taste for obscure bands (pretty rebellious stuff at a Dave Matthews–obsessed private college), she didn't judge me. She willingly went to Guided by Voices concerts with me, which was about the most romantic thing I'd ever imagined. I was still clinging to normalcy on the outside, but I was slowly feeling more comfortable in my own skin. She empowered me to take risks, like writing about music for the local alternative weekly paper, which was the first place where my weirdness was seen as an asset, and life felt bubbly with empowerment.

Somewhere around this time the unthinkable happened—unthinkable to a repressed guy from Deshler, at least. We were walking through campus one fall afternoon, hand in hand, bundled in hoodies and jeans while leaves dropped off the trees. "I want you to share your feelings," she said.

I was probably twenty-one years old, and nobody had ever made such an insane offer. The last time I experimented with sharing was a couple years earlier. My high school friend Matt was driving with his girlfriend up front, and another girl, whom I really liked, was beside me in the backseat. "One Headlight" by The Wallflowers, one of that year's biggest hits, was playing on the radio, and the girls were discussing how much they loved it. "This song," I said, "always makes me feel really sad. That guy sounds so lonely." The discussion dropped for a beat, long enough for the music to end and a commercial for used cars to begin. Both girls laughed and started making jokes about how big of a baby I was. I remember pressing my body back into the seat, like I was trying to get so small I would disappear.

"I don't know. I'm just kind of feeling, I don't know, like *sad*?" I said, holding her hand, the sharp breeze swaying her yellow ponytail. "It's stupid. Never mind."

"No, I want to hear."

I explained that one of my roommates had hurt my feelings. But I said it was my fault, because I shouldn't have my feelings hurt. Meaning: normal people don't have feelings. There was a nervous energy in my chest after sharing. I was half expecting the girls from

Matt's car to drive by laughing or the nearby payphone to ring and a Korn song to be blasting through its receiver. Instead, she kissed me and said that sounded hard and she was sorry. She said I should always share my feelings.

My chest felt a lightness. Not a full-on weightlessness or anything transcendent, but maybe more like I had been lugging a basket full of rocks throughout my life. Sharing my feelings suddenly meant that one of those rocks clacked to the ground. It seemed that every time after that day, whenever I expressed myself instead of being self-deprecating or holding it in, another rock fell from the basket and it became a little easier to love myself. Clack after clack after clack until eventually in my middle twenties I finally felt truly comfortable in my own skin. It was all thanks to her.

Not that I completely appreciated it at the time. I briefly broke up with her during our senior year. I was still learning to be comfortable with myself, I think, and one day just called off the relationship. We got back together after graduation, but our spark seemed dull or maybe even gone. I think I knew this at the time, but I just held on to my skill for smiling, and shrugging, and carrying on as if everything were normal. Our relationship continued to feel okay as we graduated and began a life together.

››››››

Pema Chödrön would be proud of me today. I am now past the hopeless stage of my divorce and have moved onto the arguing-about-who-gets-the-dented-2010-Hyundai-with-the-missing-door-handle stage. Tibetan Buddhism doesn't seem to mention whether debating who keeps the Fartmobile is the beginning of the middle or the middle of the beginning or what. But I'll take it.

It's all part of the process of beginning again, something I have never been comfortable doing. I was always crawling back to my abusive teenage friends because I was afraid to start over. I was always clinging to my broken romantic relationships for the same reason. Now, staring at the kitchen utensils that I thought would make me feel whole again, I have no choice but to start over. Often, it's at these breaking points that we find the clarity or strength to try something new. Some would call it desperation; others would say it's beginning again.

20
BRING US TOGETHER AGAIN

"Last fall the president turned up, and if Deshler, now without a historical marker, were to erect one it probably would read: 'Harry Truman Spoke Here,'" David Dempsey wrote about Deshler in 1949.

Update: They never did that, and, currently, the only historical marker in town denotes a few citizens who played professional baseball and all our past winners of the Tomato Queen pageant. But Dempsey was right; maybe we should highlight how this microscopic town has been a hotbed of presidential stopovers. Starting in 1899 and rolling on through Ronald Reagan, Deshler welcomed six presidents and a seventh if you count Warren G. Harding's body, whose casket passed by on a train en route to his burial in Marion, Ohio. All of them arrived via those same rails that were laid in the late 1800s and helped convert the Great Black Swamp into this agricultural powerhouse. While I will always be weirdly partial to Reagan's 1984 visit—when I was four years old and drew a sign for him—Richard Nixon's stop in Deshler (featuring a very different sign) was easily the most consequential for the country and for Lake Erie.

››››››

Less than a month before the 1968 general election, Nixon was desperate for votes and looking to shift gears on his campaign. This battle had been one of the most intense in the country's history, a byproduct of the chaotic social climate that saw Dr. Martin Luther King Jr. and Robert Kennedy both assassinated within the previous twelve months, not to mention the nation ripping itself apart over the Vietnam War.

By fall, only a few percentage points separated Nixon from Democratic nominee Hubert Humphrey. Complicating the mix was an independent candidate, segregationist and Alabama governor George Wallace. Much like when Truman ran in '48, a controversial third candidate from the Deep South was mangling election predictions. True, Wallace was siphoning Dixiecrat votes from Humphrey, but the theory was that he was also keeping Nixon from securing states like Florida. The election was being called a dead heat, and Nixon's campaign needed a spark. It needed growth and change and probably a miracle if he was to ascend to the White House, because experts said Humphry would likely cruise into the lead any day now. Nixon was feeling hopeless.

Infamously, he tried guest-starring on the top-rated show on television, the Day-Glo, hippy-dippy sketch comedy program *Laugh-In*. In a nonsensical switchboard operator bit, Nixon's awkward face, heavily covered in pancake makeup, turns to the camera and asks, "Sock it to me?" According to producer George Schlatter, those four words took an excruciating six takes to film. Not that it mattered, as this awkward cameo didn't seem to help Nixon's poll numbers, and so he was sent back to the drawing board, looking everywhere for a new edge.

He found that edge in the least edgy place in America.

On the morning of October 22, eighth-grader Vicki Lynne Cole was looking forward to getting out of school because she'd heard you could volunteer to be a Nixonette when the presidential candidate's train stopped in Deshler later. Cole, with a dark bob haircut and thick black glasses, the daughter of a minister and a schoolteacher, reported to the town's one-story brick firehouse for her free uniform: a red, white, and blue paper Nixonette dress that slipped over her normal clothes.

The editor of the *Deshler Flag* later described the weather as being "as windy and dusty as I've ever seen. I saw campaign hats and signs flying straight down Main Street and out into the fields."

"When the train stopped, everyone surged forward and I dropped my [original] sign," Cole said. Her original sign read: "LBJ Convinced Us to Vote Republican." Frantic, she weaved her way toward the other Nixonettes near the front of the crowd and saw people walking over a discarded white sign on the pavement. Without thinking, she grabbed it before joining the other girls. Cole didn't care what it said, she just wanted to have something to wave through the air like the other kids; she just wanted to belong to the group.

The new sign read: BRING US TOGETHER AGAIN.

Nixon's train had pulled into Deshler at 6:55 p.m. sharp, just as the sun dropped into the horizon and the deep autumn chill set in with that vicious wind. On the rear platform of the last railcar, State Senator Howard Cook introduced the Ohio Senate hopeful William

Saxbe, who said a few words and welcomed the main attraction: former Vice President Richard Milhous Nixon.

Nixon told the modest crowd that in the forty-five minutes since his train left Lima, one murder, two rapes, and forty-five major crimes of violence had occurred in this country. The crowd was likely not surprised by the information, because any time Nixon was near a microphone, it seemed, he'd been trying to spook everyone with talk of murderers and robbers roaming free. He could probably see the bored faces in Deshler. They were the same faces he had been staring at across the country as interest in his candidacy continued to fade. Nixon was in trouble, and this tired fire-and-brimstone routine was not helping matters.

With a full-bodied wave goodbye, he retreated into the caboose, and the train began its hourlong journey to Toledo.

This stop was nothing to Nixon. It meant so little that the official schedule misspelled the town's name. But soon, this meaningless Deshler speech dramatically shifted the election in his favor, because during that toothless doom-and-gloom speech, one of Nixon's team spotted Vicki Lynne Cole.

"I was then a speechwriter on the campaign train, whistle-stopping through Deshler, Ohio, when a Nixon aide, the mature straight-arrow Dick Moore, stuck his head in my compartment to say he saw that sign," Nixon campaign writer Jonathan Weisman said. "I put it in a statement at the next whistle-stop and—boom!—it became a big deal."

Almost overnight, his speeches ditched the crime angle for national unity. He frequently used the phrase "Bring Us Together Again." This fresh topic seemed to resonate with crowds. Nixon acknowledged what a turbulent year it had been and that he alone could fix it—he alone could bring us together.

Voters loved the message, and they especially loved it whenever he mentioned Vicki Lynne Cole from some little town nobody had ever heard of.

Soon, polling suggested Nixon's campaign had, in fact, begun all over. Here was the spark he had been craving. On the strength of this message, Nixon held off a late charge from Humphrey, winning the White House by only five hundred thousand votes.

The new president mentioned Vicki Lynne Cole and Deshler by name in his acceptance speech, and reporters soon flocked to the former Great Black Swamp for an interview. The Cole family had to unplug the phone at night so they could sleep. Once, Vicki was sequestered in the principal's office so classes at Deshler Elementary wouldn't be any more disrupted than they already had been. The *Flag*'s editor, Paul Scharf, was made de facto publicist, and all requests went through him.

"[Deshler] stood almost invisible in its lonely place among the corn fields Thursday, nearly hidden by the dreary autumn mists," said the *Toledo Blade*. "Yet the eyes of the nation were focusing briefly on this small farming community, and its residents blushingly sensed the immensity of this gaze."

"I was probably the shyest thirteen-year-old ever," Cole said, reflecting many years later. "During my first television interview, I was shaking so bad I thought I would pass out. Then I guess I got used to it, and it was fun."

In January, she participated in the inauguration parade in Washington, D.C., rolling down Pennsylvania Avenue on a float with the popular chorale group Up with People. Vicki was bundled in a coat and a white fur hat, waving her iconic sign. Bring Us Together Again.

"I just look at the whole thing this way," barber Richard Burner told a reporter while cutting the hair of one of Vicki's classmates. "When any big shots ever came to Deshler before, they never remembered much. Two minutes outside of town they probably asked, 'What did you say the name of that place was?' But it didn't happen that way this time....[Nixon] has really made us feel important, and I don't know if things will ever be quite the same for Deshler."

Burner, who was also my barber as a child, was incorrect. Seemingly, the whole town blocked this event from memory. Things maybe even overcorrected back toward normalcy, probably thanks to the Watergate scandal.

Within a few years, nobody in Deshler talked about Nixon's embrace of our town. I was never told the story of Tricky Dick coming here or of Vicki Lynne Cole, despite the fact that it happened only ten years before I was born.

Say what you will about Richard Nixon, but this vanishing act of local history is a shame. Maybe the Great Black Swamp, though it has been extinct for more than a century, is still strong enough to swallow memories whole like so many horses and wagons and hopes. We should talk more about stuff like this, otherwise our ambivalence erases not only memories but also prevents pride, until a place feels wide open and empty.

If anything, Nixon proves that this place can also be a place of rebirth. A place where hopelessness is the beginning of the beginning. Just look at Lake Erie in the '70s and Nixon's surprising relationship to its water.

21
AMERICA'S DEAD SEA

After Northwest Ohio's corn production shot up in the 1960s, all that fertilizer went, of course, to Lake Erie. However, when it got there, the runoff was hardly even noticed. That's because the lake had a lot of other pollutants to deal with at the time. It turns out 2014 was far from the first time Lake Erie had turned toxic.

By the end of the 1960s, the Cuyahoga River in Cleveland had famously caught fire, and Lake Erie, which it fed into, had grown so polluted that it earned a grim nickname: America's Dead Sea. In 1969, NBC produced a special called "Who Killed Lake Erie?" Before Johnny Carson had probably ever even heard of John Denver, he took a jab at Northwest Ohio, monologuing, "Lake Erie? Isn't that where fish go to die?" In 1971, even beloved children's book author Dr. Seuss kicked us while we were down in *The Lorax*.

> In search of some water that isn't so smeary
> I hear things are just as bad up in Lake Erie.

None of these attacks were off the mark. The lake was overrun with debris, silt, and dead and decaying aquatic life. Harbors were "continuously and characteristically foul, unpleasant, and odorous," one scientist noted. Beaches were routinely closed during the 1960s and '70s due to toxic water concerns. Most troubling: oxygen levels were so depleted that great patches of the lake were considered scientifically "dead," and several species of fish vanished.

"This is Lake Erie," *Science News* reported. "A wasteland, a lifeless body of water that has lost its sparkle and vitality and is being hastened to its wretched, fetid death by man's affluent wastes."

Princeton Professor Richard Falk said, "The lake has become virtually an inert mass, useful for transportation, dangerous for health, useless for life-support."

Surprisingly, agriculture was not blamed as a major culprit, despite things like a 1969 article titled "Man's Influence on Lake Erie," which noted that since 1963 (about the first growing season after *Crop Economics for Ohio* was published), phosphorus had increased by 50 percent in the lake. Instead, people focused on municipal and industrial polluters like the phosphate detergent industry, which was switching its focus to brewing up rust inhibiters and their pollutant byproducts. So, when experts pointed fingers in every direction except agriculture, they weren't entirely wrong.

The sewage of nine million people was being dumped into Lake Erie, sometimes untreated, other times treated with a chlorine mixture that itself was toxic. Also, an estimated 186 industries also flushed their wastewater into the lake. Scientists found alarming levels of DDT, polychlorinated biphenyls (PCBs), dioxins, heavy metals, asbestos, radium, mirex, ammonia, and phenols, among other substances. Scarier still was the fact that far worse toxic chemicals were being created when two or more of these contaminants combined in the water. News footage from the era shows bile-colored waterways clogged with trash and debris. The lakeshores were posted with signs saying DANGER POLLUTED WATER—NO SWIMMING with a skull and crossbones neatly painted beside the bold type. Garbage and dead fish washed up on the shores, and one newspaper even featured a picture of what appeared to be a rusted pickup truck half submerged in the water. Some rivers that fed into Erie were estimated to have 1,500 times the human safety level of bacteria.

But it's surprising agriculture wasn't at least garnering part of the focus. "These modern agricultural landscapes have been stabilized and sanitized; the soils are transformed from living systems to growing mediums," Cain Blythe and Paul Jepson explain. And everything that went into that transformation was carried straight to the lake: "A big part of Toledo's problem comes from the Maumee River," *The Wall Street Journal* reported, "which drains a broad swath of agricultural land, feeding the bloom on Toledo's end of the lake. Other major cities near the Great Lakes such as Chicago and Detroit haven't experienced similar restrictions."

Once again, Northwest Ohio's runoff was proving to be the absolute worst thing to drain into the absolute worst place it could. You could literally see this happening: "From the air on the day after a good rain, a gull or a pilot can see a huge billow of brown mud extending far into the lake from the mouth of the Maumee River," *Cleveland Magazine* noted. "That plume of mud carries the fertilizer that feeds Lake Erie's persistent, strangling algae."

Yet the overall focus on agriculture's pollution was limited, and farmers were actually assured that they were *not* contributing. In a 1970 article, Ohio State University professors and agronomists

Garth Volk and Leonard Baver suggested that Northwest Ohio's dense clay soil makes it impervious to fertilizer pollution. "[The soil] is relatively insoluble and thereby is quite resistant to leaching....Only a small percentage of the applied phosphate is eroded from the land and reaches Lake Erie." They did note, however, that this was largely speculation on their part. "Reliable data are so meager as to changes in phosphorus input from rural land sources over time that they do not permit accurate appraisal of whether the present contribution from such sources is much greater than from pristine land surfaces."

Regardless of its source, the total amount of phosphorus in Lake Erie had risen 700 percent since the 1800s, reaching twenty-four thousand tons of phosphorus by the end of the 1960s. According to a National Commission on Water Quality report, Lake Erie had aged fifteen thousand years in the two hundred years since pioneers first settled on its shores.

"By speeding up the aging process with industrial and municipal wastes, man has polluted Erie to the point where today it is like a child with progeria—that rare disease that accelerates the life cycle so the victim may die of old age at 10," wrote Casey Bukro in the *Chicago Tribune*.

Enter our strange new hero: Deshler's number one fan, Richard Nixon.

"In 1972 [Nixon] signed the Clean Water Act which contained sweeping changes. For the first time in US history it declared a legal intent to restore and maintain aquatic ecosystems," Sharon Levy writes. "It transferred authority over effluents from sewage treatment plants and industrial wastewaters from the states to the federal EPA and set a wildly idealistic goal that all such discharges into US waters should cease by 1985."

But let's not get ahead of ourselves. The president only seems heroic on paper. "The Nixon administration was apoplectic" about the bill, notes one historian. Congress passed the environmentally forward-thinking bill, but Nixon vetoed it. Both the Senate and House voted to override the president's veto, and the Clean Water Act (CWA) was forced into law on October 18, 1972.

The law implemented pollution control programs like setting wastewater standards for industry. The EPA also developed national water quality criteria recommendations for pollutants in surface waters. The most important element was that the Clean Water Act made it unlawful to discharge any pollutant from a point source into navigable waters unless a permit was obtained. Nixon felt forced into founding the EPA, which he had done two years prior, and signing the CWA and responded to this watershed environmental moment by appointing corporate execs to every role in the National Pollution Control Council. Willingly or not, Nixon will go down in history as the president who saved Lake Erie the first time it needed saving. Good and bad. Light and dark. A villain and hero if ever there was one.

Despite the president's best efforts to destroy the Clean Water Act, it went into effect and the unthinkable happened: it quickly brought Lake Erie back from the dead. "In less than a decade," says Dan Egan, "the algae blooms shrank by 50%, and even Dr. Seuss issued an apology and revised his text."

By 1981, *Cleveland Magazine*'s Nancy Kool noted, "The lakes and their tributaries are visibly cleaner. Foot-wide grease balls no longer bob in the Detroit River, and ducks do not die after landing there. DDT levels in all the lakes have declined faster than expected, and the same is true for many other contaminants." She added, "Phosphorus levels have dropped accordingly."

"The miracle is that it worked," an optimistic *Nautical Quarterly* article added. "Lake Erie beaches are open for swimming, the worst industrial discharge problems have been remedied, and the majority of municipal sewage treatment plants meet current water quality standards."

This was a victory virtually unprecedented in American ecological history. Environmental damage that had effectively killed one of the largest freshwater bodies on Earth was reversed due to legislation, buy-in from corporations, and the passion of citizens. This was a titanic win for the growing environmental movement and the public's consciousness about our planet.

In an alternate timeline, you could mention this social justice victory in the same breath as Rachel Carson's *Silent Spring* or the bald eagle coming back from the endangered species list. This should have been the spark where everything changed for the better, a victory with a domino effect of healing other types of air, water, and land pollution. The Clean Water Act should have kept Lake Erie safe for eternity. But we know that's not the timeline we live in. We know the lake doglegged hard from this victory, and the water quality worsened to the point where the 2014 algae outbreak happened. Even though we know that particular outbreak began largely because of agricultural runoff, the EPA shouldn't have let it get that bad, right?

It's at this point that our real villain steps out of the shadows and into the daylight. Two villains, in fact.

22

SHE COULD KICK A BEAR TO DEATH WITH HER BARE FEET

There's a photo of me at age four leaning against a window on Deshler's Main Street, towheaded and tiny, smiling proudly beside a huge sign that my preschool class spent all week drawing with crayons. It reads: WELCOME RONALD REAGAN.

I look pretty excited, and I was not the only one. The entire town was abuzz that fall of 1984, sixteen years after Nixon visited. That afternoon Reagan was scheduled to stop in Deshler on what would be one of the last whistle-stop presidential tours in our nation's history. That day, he would speak to over one hundred thousand people spread out across several Black Swamp towns, including the home of the Worst Road in America, Perrysburg. I recall getting bored with all the standing around and waiting, so I asked my grandma to take me home. That means I missed the president giving his speech from the back of the same railcar Truman used when in Deshler, the *Ferdinand Magellan*, pitching his "Morning in America" message. It was an idealistic campaign that claimed that our country was, to quote his wildly popular and folksy political ad at the time, "Stronger, prouder, and better than it was just four years ago." While this ad and Reagan's speeches around the time reference lower inflation and job numbers, they do not mention whether Lake Erie was better off than it was four years ago, back in 1980, when the former film star of *Bedtime for Bonzo* first came to power.

"New anti-environmental conservatives in the Republican Party found a champion in Ronald Reagan," notes the *American Journal of Public Health*. "As president-elect, he snubbed a moderate environmental policy blueprint drafted by Republican environmentalists in favor of a plan written by the Heritage Foundation, a right-wing think tank then less than a decade old, that devolved EPA functions and authority back to the state."

When Reagan took office, it probably felt like Lake Erie's upward trajectory would continue indefinitely, but the new commander-in-chief had other ideas. In Reagan's first round of budgets, aid for the Great Lakes dropped from about $22 million to just over $2 million. A nearly 90 percent slashing.

The new president's actions against regulation and the environment were swift. "The only planning agency concerned with all the lakes, The Great Lakes Basin Commission, has been abolished," Nancy Kool warned. "The Reagan administration moves promise to magnify the EPA's weaknesses and nullify its strengths."

Nowhere was this more consequential than with Anne Gorsuch. Gorsuch, a thirty-eight-year-old Colorado attorney and legislator, was appointed head of the EPA by Reagan. She opposed the Clean Air Act, water quality rules, and hazardous waste protections. According to the *Washington Post*, the new leader of the Environmental Protection Agency "wore fur coats and smoked two packs of Marlboros a day; her government-issued car got about fifteen miles per gallon of gasoline." The *Rocky Mountain News* once said, "She could kick a bear to death with her bare feet."

The EPA's first administrator, William Ruckelshaus, said that she treated a lot of people in the agency as the enemy. "Gorsuch demoralized, marginalized, and reorganized EPA staff...reducing staff at the agency by 21 percent between 1981 and 1983...dissolving the Office of Enforcement," writes the *American Journal of Public Health*. "In the first year of the new administration, civil enforcement cases fell by about three quarters." She also appointed executives from the industries they were tasked with regulating, such as the heads of Aerojet General and Exxon. Albert Kendricks was named as the next administrator of the EPA's Chicago office, despite the fact that his current job was supervising safety and environmental protection for agribusiness giant Monsanto. Gorsuch once boasted that she had reduced the thickness of the book of clean water regulations from six inches to a half inch.

A 1982 *Doonesbury* comic features an EPA employee sitting on a building ledge, considering suicide, while Anne Gorsuch can be overheard firing employees from within the building.

Eventually, even Reagan grew tired of the negative publicity, and she resigned.

In the 1986 memoir *Are You Tough Enough?* Gorsuch said: "I was not the first to receive his special brand of benevolent neglect, a form of conveniently looking the other way, while his staff continues to do some very dirty work."

She seems right, because the dirty work was far from done. These rollbacks and slashings continued, just under far less dramatic circumstances. By the time Ronald Reagan visited Deshler in 1984, water quality had already taken a huge step backward. *The Journal of Soil and Water Conservation* reported that the groundwater in Northwest Ohio was the worst in the state, worse than Rust Belt behemoths like Cleveland and Akron. Seventeen species of fish were now known to be extinct from the Maumee River and another twenty-six teetered on the verge.

Weirdly, Lake Erie still appeared healthy on the surface. Since the advent of the Clean Water Act, swimming and fishing returned without much concern from Northwest Ohioans. Everything seemed so normal, in fact, that nobody worried much about these cuts. Beneath the surface, water quality was reverting to its toxic 1960s state. Since the federal government had all but bailed on environmental interests, most meaningful decisions were made by a ragtag conglomeration of the governors of states bordering the lakes. This meant that the Great Lakes' fate was left in the "hands of eight squabbling states whose abuse of the water brought the lakes to the edge of death nearly a decade ago," Kool wrote, comparing the governors' ability to cooperate to an episode of *Family Feud* without the laughs and prize money. "The lakes are also threatened by the recent public perception that 'Lake Erie has been saved' and the lakes' future is secure, a delusion as comfortable and as dangerous as the myth that the lakes are limitless and indestructible."

Dr. Charles Herdendorf, then director of the Center for Lake Erie Area Research, agreed, noting, "When you start cleaning up a lake, it's easy to do the first things; but then the curve begins to flatten out, and it becomes harder to make gains. In terms of phosphorus control, it costs more and more money in relation to what you achieve."

Since federal money had pretty much vanished, those stakeholding states were not only bickering but also broke. The manufacturing boom of the twentieth century was over, and Rust Belt economic realities had grown dire. Nurturing Lake Erie was not a high priority with so many industrial cities imploding and those citizens hitting hard times. It was, sadly, exactly the kind of moment a federal agency like the EPA was built for handling if it were fully funded.

"Unless steps are taken now to halt the present tide of pollution and the more than doubling of the load by the year 2020," Herdendorf predicted in an essay, "the pollution problems in Lake Erie will increase accordingly."

Unfortunately, the water quality did exactly as he predicted. One EPA report noted a litany of sins, such as how the Ottawa River, which feeds into the Maumee, had a "no-contact" advisory during that time span, meaning people weren't even supposed to let their skin touch it. The EPA also noted the river's fish had tumors and other deformities, as well as the overall degradation of wildlife and water quality.

It's here where our story finds its villains and the timeline finally locks into place. It's as crystal clear as Lake Erie's water once was that all our efforts to conquer and deforest the Great Black Swamp led directly to a million acres of farmland springing up in the twentieth century. And we know that a push to farm corn on a massive scale, and saturate it all with fertilizer, collided with Ronald Reagan's decision to stop supporting the Clean Water Act and the EPA, which continued the slow degradation of the lake's water quality. Several subsequent administrations kept funds for both low. Add this to the rising water temperature of Lake Erie between 1980 and today, and we get 2014's toxic algae outbreak.

It comes as no surprise that people like me felt so disconnected to this place. It would take something far greater than Richard Nixon to bring us together this time.

23
FIRE AND WATER

To my great disappointment, there's no mention of The Firebugs when I drive into tiny Evansport, Ohio.

The town's only historical marker denotes that it reached peak size in 1880 (population 300) and spends a large chunk of the plaque ironically praising the fire department's history. It fails to mention a gristmill and sawmill in town that caught fire in the late 1800s due to "suspicious circumstances," according to one town history I found before visiting. There is also nothing about historian Louis Simonis's 1979 reflection, "In the middle 1880s, new lights and sounds came from the Tiffin River; not the promising brilliance and din of speculation but the awesome light of burning mills—dam splitting dynamite charges echoed through the canyons of the Tiffin River. Lockport, Evansport, the mills burned; the dams were blown out." He continues, "It was not until 1903 that convictions were made in reference to the burning of mills at Lockport and Evansport."

Those convictions were for a group of arsonists-for-hire known in the media as The Firebugs. Homes, barns, businesses, and more were set ablaze for nearly two decades around Northwest Ohio. According to the *Cincinnati Enquirer*, so many fires had happened around Evansport that by 1903, all major insurance carriers had stopped issuing policies to the area. Eventually, over one hundred conspirators were arrested for their roles in an arson insurance scam that caused over $1.5 million in damages, adding up to over $52 million today. While this was headline-grabbing stuff at the time, it has all but faded from the collective Northwest Ohio consciousness, like so many other interesting stories that can tell us just as much about ourselves as our history.

Just outside of town, probably about where one of these mills once stood, is the newly minted Weisgerber-Pohlmann Nature Preserve: seventy-five acres of often flooded farmland that the Black Swamp Conservancy purchased and is in the process of returning to its natural state. Someday, it will look more like that lost swampland before the 1800s, but today it gives off the vibe of a construction site. Melanie Coulter explains how her organization recently ripped out the corrugated plastic drainage tiles and purposefully reshaped the land to populate it with native species of grasses, wildflowers, and trees that will hopefully have a powerful impact on the ecological health of Northwest Ohio. Today, it's mostly raw soil and tall grasses, dotted with tiny pink flags each denoting a recently planted sapling. These plants, along with newly carved ridges and eddies, wrap along this crescent-shaped curve of land along the Tiffin River.

It might not look like much, but this land is currently working very hard.

The river measures maybe twenty feet across and about five feet deep, give or take some rainfall, and is filled with water that is, as

Melanie puts it, "mocha brown." Northwest Ohio's waterways were not naturally all this pale, muddy color. That Mississippi River complexion is, in fact, due to all the farm runoff. Millions and millions of gallons of water, leaving behind their silt and other contaminants. This particular stretch of the Tiffin River is a funnel point for several area farms, whose runoff has been passing through here on its way to Lake Erie for generations.

Getting the area's water back to a pure, clear state is the Black Swamp Conservancy's goal with projects like this. Ideally, a native environment will filter water through the earth, and the plants that thrive on phosphorus will gobble up the potentially troublesome element before the water eventually passes cleanly downstream and into Lake Erie. The theory is that even global warming's rise in water temperature won't be a problem for Lake Erie because it won't possess all the phosphorus that gets converted to toxic algae.

"In ecological terms, the muck and still water of the Great Black Swamp wasn't a wasteland at all," writes Dan Egan. "It was Lake Erie's kidney, a grand filtering system that turned muddy rainwater flushing off the land into crystalline flows by the time they reached the lake."

If today's Northwest Ohio were an actual human kidney, it would be very close to needing dialysis or outright removal.

It'll take a lot more than just this Evansport tract to rescue Lake Erie. The Black Swamp Conservancy currently maintains 145 tracts of land around Northwest Ohio, totaling more than nineteen thousand acres. And still, it's a drop in the bucket. The greatest need is for more strategic wetland revitalization near hot spots like this where large amounts of phosphorus pass unfiltered into the waterways. But that's a big challenge, because while some of the land is donated, the bulk of the organization's property is purchased from farmers. Farmers, for obvious reasons, aren't usually too eager to turn over a portion of land that makes money year-in and year-out for a modest one-time payment, even when it's in the interest of ecological good.

Even though Melanie is upbeat and enthusiastic about the difference her group is making, there's a numbness inside me. Their uphill battle, multiplied by my difficulty in connecting to this place, makes me eager to drive home, even though my son is with his mom this week and my home is now empty.

Walking back from the river and toward our cars, we find a strange muddy patch among the crusty, dry dirt. It captures our attention because pretty much everywhere else within the confines of the Preserve has been baked dry by the sun.

"Huh," Melanie muses, haunching down toward a trickle of water. "I thought this was a leaky drainage tile we missed, but now I'm not so sure." We follow the mud to its source and discover a small, clear pool. At its center is a gentle gurgling, bubbling rush of water. "I think this might be a natural spring," she says, delighted and awed. "It probably hasn't flowed for 100, 150 years."

I plunge in my hand up to the elbow. It's cold and shocking and calming.

Something shifts inside me. A shift away from all the disappointment and ambivalence I've been lugging around for so long. I don't see it at that exact moment, but that hardwired need to shrug, and smile, and carry on like normal fades away. It's never done me any good.

Both Lake Erie and I do not know the future, and not knowing the future is scary. But there's a need to face scary things in order to avoid the mistakes of the past.

PART IV

Tragedy is not hopeless. Tragedy cleanses man.
I believe that only through spiritual crisis healing begins.
—Andrei Tarkovsky

24

YOU NEVER FORGET YOUR FIRST TOXIC ALGAE

The first time I get to see toxic green algae is the summer after Evansport. My divorce has been finalized, and I've become a happier and more confident person. Beginning again has not been without its pitfalls, but it's a process I've come to enjoy. My future is unknown, but for the first time in a long time that looks good.

Lake Erie, on the other hand, does not look so good. It's August 2023 and the water is a pale, moldy green. Not the eye-catching Verde Alpi, kale-shake green I was expecting. But nonetheless, toxic. The National Oceanic and Atmospheric Administration's Lake Erie Harmful Algal Bloom Tracker tells me today is the highest toxicity the water has seen in a year, which is why I have returned to Maumee Bay State Park's beach. The moss-colored water hits the shore in lazy, small waves. The big wooden signs are still standing tall, warning us not to touch any water that looks puked up by the little girl in *The Exorcist*.

The sun is high and strong, but it's not as brutal as the last time I was here. The mildewed, fishy smell from before is also gone, and the air simply smells like nothing at all. A few people are sunbathing, and surprisingly large tents for a charity event are being erected farther down the sand. Despite the toxic water, Toledo hasn't lost its ability to carry on like everything's normal.

Down by the edge of the parking lot, I wander toward a guy pulling a surfboard from his truck bed and unfurling a sail. "You going windsurfing?" I ask.

"I'm gonna attempt it." He looks out of place in Toledo, wearing board shorts and a lightweight swimming shirt. He is probably a decade older than me, judging by the deep creases on his tanned face, but he has the youthful, disheveled hair of a California surfer boy.

"Are you worried about the algae at all?"

"No. I was out Monday, and I didn't see any algae. If it's bad, it looks like pea soup." He pulls out a second board and sail rig, telling me that his buddy is also meeting him for a quick ride. He begins explaining the finer points of a north wind versus a westward wind. Today's a westward one and not as good as he'd like, which seems to be his biggest concern.

"So, this isn't toxic algae?"

"Nah, that's just the sun," he says.

"There's no danger of getting sick from the algae? I just saw that sign over there and it scared me." I point to the water.

"We're gonna find out," he laughs. "But I'm not going swimming in it. And if things go right, I won't touch it."

"Knock on wood."

We share a laugh and I look back over my shoulder.

AVOID SWALLOWING LAKE WATER.

Meteorologist Joe Astolfi would probably have stronger words for this guy than "knock on wood." Just this morning Astolfi published an article about HABs on Lake Erie. His report says the patch I am currently looking at spans about three hundred square miles, roughly the size of New York City's five boroughs. Its toxicity is about half as potent as in 2014, due to lower precipitation this year. However, Astolfi warns: "It is advised to avoid going in the water, as these areas are most hazardous to humans and animals."

I don't stick around to watch the windsurfing. I hop in my Prius, having lost the battered old Hyundai in the divorce. I spend the rest of the afternoon following the Harmful Algal Bloom Tracker, which is color coded kind of like a meteorologist's hurricane prediction map. Wandering along Lake Erie's shore and looking for greener, deadlier algae, I feel a bit like I did in high school. Once again, I'm driving around Northwest Ohio, feeling rejected and listening to noisy, awkward music, but there's a new strength I didn't have back then. A comfort that only comes from enduring the most painful tragedy of my life. Ironically, I don't think I would have been able to evolve to this confident point if not for my ex.

After college, we moved to Arizona and Portland, Oregon, where we got married at a place called Voodoo Doughnuts. Before the wedding, all of our friends threw a surprise engagement party for us, and it was the most loved I had felt since being a child. All throughout our marriage, I kept talking about my feelings and inching closer to being the artistic weirdo I dreamed about becoming while reading *Come as You Are*. I wasn't fully there yet in my twenties, though. I was still kind of embarrassed by expressing myself, despite doing some pretty neat things like being a rock critic for weekly papers and small magazines and finally starting a band. We were called Clap Amp and played noisy, punky dance music. Our biggest gig was at a bar located beneath a funeral home and was attended by maybe a dozen people.

Eventually, we settled in her hometown of Louisville, Kentucky, where I felt we sort of evolved into the best versions of ourselves. We had a son, I began a writing career, and she quit working in corporate HR in favor of flipping houses for a living. I was finally fully comfortable with my emotions, the family chef and stay-at-home dad for a few years, and she fixed up our home and managed our finances. I joined an improv group, and she became deeply interested in researching exotic but cheap beach vacations to places like the Abacos. It was a good and unique, but often stressful, life.

This marriage was comfortable, but I was frequently unhappy. We'd become our best selves, but those were now two different people. We drifted apart and communicated badly. She drove me kind of nuts and I drove her nuts. If she laughed at one of my jokes, it surprised me because it had usually been a long time since we shared joy like that.

I didn't share this discomfort with friends, though, and I didn't see a therapist. I would often ask if she was unhappy or what was wrong, but when she said "nothing" I gratefully continued pretending everything was fine. I shrugged, and smiled, and went back to thinking this constant seasickness was normal. *This is what a long-term, stable, productive marriage looks like. Ebbs and flows. Boredom. That's a good thing*, I said to myself. *You're so lucky.*

And I was lucky. It was a great life, and I tried hard to acknowledge that fact frequently. I gave her lots of hugs and kisses and I love yous, and I meant them. I felt like I loved her more in this period than ever, and I loved our imperfection. By the time she declared that she no longer loved me, I was fully invested in this relationship for life. It came as a shock and was the hardest thing that ever happened to me, but hitting rock bottom was also starting to feel like the *best* thing that ever happened to me. With a little distance, I can see now that it wasn't one shocking explosion that sunk our boat; rather it was like we kept accumulating little rocks, one by one, ignoring them as they piled into the boat and eventually took it underwater. While I was losing rocks of inhibition, I was gaining new ones elsewhere. This divorce was a product of both of our decisions. It had stopped working years before either of us actually acknowledged we were in trouble.

Standing alone on Lake Erie's shore, just out of reach of the cyanobacteria-laced green algae, I see this new version of myself more clearly. I exercise, I go to therapy, I take anxiety medicine. I have made a conscious effort not to shrug, not to just smile, and not to carry on like everything's fine when it's not. That feels good.

Today's toxic algae journey takes me as far east as the Davis-Besse Nuclear Power Station, which sits beside the Magee Marsh wetlands, a hot spot for all the warblers migrating through in the spring and fall. The walk toward the coastline is dotted with black-eyed Susans, and the cloudless day illuminates that mossy green algae as it gently coats the rocks. The urge to touch it is high, but I resist.

You can see the power plant's enormous hourglass-shaped cooling towers from this little rocky beach. It makes me think of the line-dancing retirees Les and Pam. Maybe they were onto something with their theory about it having something to do with Lake Erie's problems? Not exactly, but they weren't wrong to be worried, either. A friend recently sent me a 2002 *Washington Post* article: "Heard About the Near-Accident at the Ohio Nuclear Plant? I'm Not Surprised." Apparently, the Davis-Besse plant almost had a Chernobyl-like meltdown that year. Rust had eaten away at its reactor pressure vessel, creating a hole wide and deep enough to put your fist into. According to former Nuclear Regulatory Commission Chief Victor Gilinsky, "Corrosion had reduced 70 pounds of steel, half a foot thick, to rust. All that was left to contain the reactor's highly pressurized supply of cooling water around the reactor core was a three-eighths inch liner of stainless steel, and the liner had started to bulge ominously." Apparently, the bulge was caught just before it was too late. Everything got fixed, and the government barely made a peep about a near-catastrophe that could have been enormous in terms of public safety as well as the future of the nuclear industry.

I don't talk to another person the rest of the day. Maybe I should be collecting more horror stories, but since the divorce I'm not so eager to experience other people's suffering. Also, it's a weekday and all the shorelines are pretty empty, lending a postapocalyptic desolation to Lake Erie and its algae. At every stop, my journey is undercut with that strange sensation of finally getting what I wanted. *Here's some deadly green algae, now what?* I thought this story would be a little cleaner. I thought the algae would be more dramatic and the swamps would be terrifying. I thought this story would have evil villains and valiant good guys. Most of all, I really thought there would be a solution. It gnaws on me, that lack of any clear path forward. How is it that we live in such an advanced society but we can't solve the problem of green slime returning every year to try to poison the drinking water?

Thankfully, other people are way further along in this thinking. There are those who would never dream of pretending everything is normal. There are people with an eye focused clearly on the future, trying to make a difference on Lake Erie. The problem is, the deck seems to be stacked against them.

25
LAKE ERIE IS NOT A TOILET

Sometimes I miss Glenn Colerider's guidance, and thanks to uncovering a digital version deep within the bowels of the PBS website, I have returned to *The Story of the Great Black Swamp* often since Bowling Green. I even once got my hands on the original script and the actual visual slides used in the production. But it wasn't as illuminating as I'd hoped. I seem to have wrung all the inspiration I can from this documentary.

I see clearly now that this film was made during that sweet spot when the Clean Water Act brought Lake Erie back from the grave but before Ronald Reagan and Anne Gorsuch took a chainsaw to the EPA. The film barely even mentions Lake Erie's health, because it was probably an afterthought at that time. This was no longer America's Dead Sea. Everything was normal here, relax. Yes, Glenn hinted at the darker truth burying us alive and "stealing the soul of everyone who touched it," but he didn't know 2014 was going to happen. And really, he was just reading cue cards.

In many ways, I've already raced past my hero. And out here, the landscape is wide open.

An interesting thing happens when we are forced to begin again. A million different possibilities suddenly open up. It's a blessing and a curse because each one of those directions is seductively liberating, but each direction is also terrifying. Every possible path into the future is almost certainly paved with mudholes and setbacks, but each offers an ecstatic flicker of hope, too.

This was the situation Lake Erie found itself in following the 2014 toxic algae outbreak. Here was a chance for a clean start, a unique moment to hit the reset button. But it was impossible to tell which solution, if any, was the best path forward. Equally liberating and infuriating was the fact that nobody seemed to be taking the lead on rehabilitating the water, so it often looked like a thousand different plans were being attempted all at once—often contradicting one another. People had good intentions, but it was often a mess.

But a mess still means people are taking action. That's agency. That's optimism. Here was a chance to begin again—again, after the Clean Water Act in the 1970s. While the EPA was better funded and more involved than it had been in the 1980s, nobody seemed to be waiting for the agency to swoop in and save the day. Instead, independent environmentalists had to discover their own paths and their own solutions.

Nowhere was the hope brighter and more innovative than with the ultraprogressive Lake Erie Bill of Rights.

"I think it's going to make everybody realize we've got to do better," Senator Sherrod Brown said about the proposed legislation. "I would hope that when 500,000 people lose their drinking water for a couple, three days, that it would have an impact on public policy not just in Ohio but around the country."

The Lake Erie Bill of Rights, which accorded the lake rights "to exist, flourish and naturally evolve," among other things, was the highest profile case in a collection of recent attempts to provide a human being's rights to an ecosystem, such as a lake, river, forest, or desert. Previously, only Venezuela and Ecuador had passed such laws. "There's no precedent for any of this," Thomas Linzey, coauthor of the bill, told *The New York Times* in 2019. "It is almost a new consciousness—that a community is not just homo sapiens."

Ironically, the bill of rights was piggybacking off the recent Citizens United Supreme Court ruling that essentially gave corporations the same rights as a human. Taking that decision as guidance, the bill of rights "entitles the lake certain rights and empowers citizens to advocate for those rights when they are being violated, like bringing legal suits against polluters."

"Much like a child, we often have someone else speak on their behalf," activist Markie Miller, another coauthor of the bill, said. "And that will become our relationship with Lake Erie. That we become trustees of this lake."

It was a revolutionary idea in America and environmentalists were, understandably, energized. This could be a new Clean Water Act but one that didn't rely on federal budgets and the whims of a frequently changing White House. Meaty write-ups in magazines and newspapers soon followed. Satirical news program *The Daily Show* even filmed a segment in Toledo, during which correspondent Michael Kosta took the idea of a lake's personhood to the extreme and held a marriage ceremony between himself and Lake Erie.

On February 26, 2019, the bill, proposed to voters as an amendment to the city charter, passed by a whopping 61 percent margin in a special election. "Beginning today," a representative from Toledoans for Safe Water said, "the people of Toledo and our allies are ushering in a new era of environmental rights by securing the rights of the Great Lake Erie." Private citizens could now take polluters to court for dumping waste into the lake, including major corporations, municipalities, and, presumably, farmers.

Once again, the former Great Black Swamp was the center of the ecological universe, but this time it was for all the right reasons. "The hope is that by beginning somewhere, like Toledo, the conversation enlarges," one proponent of the bill told *Vox*. "You never know what's going to be the tipping point."

This, however, was not that tipping point.

Despite the bill's passing, overall enthusiasm was mixed. For starters, only 9 percent of registered voters even cast a ballot for the measure. This was likely due to the underlying fact that the Lake Erie Bill of Rights was practically dead on arrival. For starters, the bill had powerful enemies. "We found out that BP was basically the sole funder of the campaign against the Lake Erie Bill of Rights," Markie Miller said during that *Daily Show* segment. "They have a refinery not far from Toledo, but I think it was more about not wanting this idea of rights of nature to take off."

I knew the exact refinery she was talking about. BP sold it to another company in 2023, but this was the same white-domed, fire-breathing location I drove past on my first trip to Toledo.

The bill's other hurdle was more public: "The initiative is a powerful tactic. And for me, coming from an activist background, it is important to send messages," City Council Member Nick Komives said. "But this is probably unconstitutional."

The day after the bill of rights passed, Drewes Farm Partnership filed a federal lawsuit claiming it violated the farm's rights. One year after that petition was filed, the Ohio State Supreme Court declared the Lake Erie Bill of Rights unconstitutional. In the end, the ruling was about as splashy and sexy as the toxic green algae that birthed it. According to the National Agricultural Law Center, the Lake Erie Bill of Rights violated the Fourteenth Amendment of the United States Constitution, which protects the right to due process. The court noted that an essential component of due process is clarity of the law. The court went on to explain that vague laws violate the Constitution because they do not provide the public with fair warning of what the law is and because they are likely to result in arbitrary enforcement from prosecutors, judges, and juries.

Not a single lawsuit was even filed in an attempt to protect Lake Erie from pollution. And each year, the toxic algae keeps returning.

This, understandably, took the wind out of the sails of environmentalists. Still, Toledo was the town too tough for toxic algae. Seemingly, this bunch of environmental optimists shrugged and smiled and got back to their new normal: looking for solutions. Some, like the nonprofit group Lake Erie Advocates, paid for a series of eye-catching billboards proclaiming "Lake Erie Is Not a Toilet," with a website hoping to organize folks into helping curb factory farming, an industry that contributed to a rise in livestock waste that was beginning to parallel phosphorus runoff in terms of damage to the ecosystem.

The Army Corps of Engineers offered a plan to capture toxic algae. "We attach billions and billions of microscopic air bubbles to the solids. It imparts buoyancy to the solids, and those solids float to the surface," a representative told NPR. "When they float to the surface, we can skim them off." While theoretically removing the lake's toxic algae (some disagree that this would remove the cyanobacteria), the plan would leave the Corps with a lot of toxic green algae sitting around, which they proposed converting into biofuel or sneakers or yoga mats. Presumably, this plan did not work out, since a recent search for "Army Corps of Engineers Yoga Mats" turned up zero hits.

One Bowling Green State University scientist began testing a theory that we should dredge up infected sediment from Toledo's ports and spread it on crops like fertilizer, creating a sort of phosphorus feedback loop.

Some suggested that we put farmers on a "nutrient diet" like the Danish government did in the 1980s. The Danes strictly limited fertilizer use in order to revive their coastal lobster population, which had been decimated by agricultural runoff. This was a promising idea for Lake Erie, considering that in less than two decades the Danish coast saw a 50 percent drop in nitrogen, a 90 percent drop in phosphorus, and a near-total rebound of lobsters. But who would police Northwest Ohio's fields? And as many farmers pointed out, they'd already slashed their fertilizer usage to the bare minimum. There wasn't much fat to lose in this nutrient diet.

There were proposals for injecting the lake water with oxygen or shocking it with hydrogen peroxide. Others recalled that back in 1957 scientists successfully exterminated toxic algae by having a crop duster sprinkle copper sulfate over a harmful bloom. However, the idea was quickly abandoned when the US National Office for Harmful Algal Blooms pointed out, "Despite the dramatic reduction in...the size of the bloom, the broad lethality of copper resulted in considerable collateral mortality of other marine organisms."

This left, really, only one option. An option that has been diligently working in the background all along: rewilding.

Rewilding was a solution that, according to ecologist Bill Mitsch, "matches the sweeping changes made to the former Black Swamp. If we're not willing to do that, we should admit we're willing to accept lakes painted bright green by blooms of cyanobacteria."

Rewilding is a scientific movement with an ecological philosophy that had been gaining traction in certain circles thanks to the fact that there is actual, verifiable scientific proof that it works to combat toxic algae. But this movement had two problems:

1. Rewilding did not result in the production of comfy yoga mats.
2. It would be an incredibly difficult, time-consuming, energy-consuming, money-consuming, goodwill-consuming effort.

But it did get results.

At its core, rewilding is as simple as it sounds. Take an area that was once a forest or a marsh or a desert but has since become, say, parking lots or farm fields or housing, and just take out the man-made elements so nature can care for itself again. Wilderness has a way of healing when given the opportunity. Entire ecosystems of plants and animals have been known to bounce back with only time and some breathing room. It's exactly the kind of work Melanie Coulter and the Black Swamp Conservancy have been doing. But their project was still too young and too small to yield the scale of scientific results necessary to curb toxic green algae on Lake Erie.

One notable rewilding success was the Dutch city of Nijmegen, famous for its claim to being the oldest city in the Netherlands at over two thousand years of age. Over thirty years ago, the city, which has a population of around 190,000, removed dikes on the River Waal. They opted to restore the natural ebbs and flows of a three-thousand-hectare floodplain and populate the space with free-roaming cattle and horses. The results included a boom in populations of beaver, sturgeon, and otters, species not seen for generations in the area. More important to the bottom-line conscious, the government saved huge sums of money, since the natural sand dunes created a buffer that meant the city no longer had to wage the frequent, and expensive, battle against flooding. In 2018, Nijmegen was awarded the prestigious European Green Capital status.

The River Waal is not an outlier. To dive into the history of rewilding is to see countless stories of animal species brought back from the brink. Eagles, coyotes, wolves, bison, a plethora of fish. However, it is far more difficult to find examples of rewilding eliminating phosphorus loads and resuscitating toxic algae infected waters. But they are out there.

Take, for example, the Everglades Agricultural Area of South Florida. What started as a nearly four-thousand-acre state-run, man-made wetland was designed to specifically capture farm runoff and proved so successful that it quickly scaled up to fifty-seven thousand acres. According Sharon Levy in *The Marsh Builders*, "Scientists working on the project demonstrated that the managed marsh could remove about 80 percent of the incoming phosphorus load."

In 2005, scientist Rob Gearheart's (no known relation to the John Denver–threatening *Toledo Blade* scribe) long-running program to use water basins and marshland to cleanse the water of the Apache Powder Company in Arizona finally began to get impressive results. After several years, the tainted groundwater went from 200 mg/l of nitrates down to only 10 mg/l, which is the federal drinking water standard.

But nobody had ever attempted to heal an ecosystem of Lake Erie's size. It's one thing to reduce the algae of a wastewater treatment center, and it's another to do it to the eleventh-largest freshwater basin on Earth.

Rewilding the Great Black Swamp would take a massive, multipronged effort just as tenacious as the efforts used to eliminate the swamp in the 1800s. Thousands of acres of Northwest Ohio farmland would need to be retrofitted back to wetland if Erie wanted a chance. That feels like a major leap for an area so indebted to agricultural production. Just like Melanie told me in Evansport, it's hard getting people to change and it's even harder getting farmers to sell productive land.

One of rewilding's champions, Bill Mitsch has been thinking about this stuff longer than just about anyone. The world has lost 87 percent of its wetlands over the last three hundred years, Mitsch told Levy. "All of these numbers are pretty shocking to me. We've got to make up for this 87 percent loss, and we're not going to do it 10 acres at a time."

Mitsch's research began in the 1970s, with a project filtering the sewage coming from a Florida trailer park through a native cypress swamp. His experiment was successful in absorbing pathogenic bacteria, organic matter, nitrogen, and phosphorus. "We discovered this ecosystem service of wetlands cleaning polluted water and interest in them exploded," he told Levy.

More recently, Mitsch and his crew have been monitoring sites in Defiance, Ohio, and Buckeye Lake. He has coined the term *wetaculture*, which he sees as a way to work alongside farmers, not in opposition to them. Mitsch's wetaculture envisions a split between rewilding the land and maintaining productive agriculture. Essentially, it involves rotating which parcels of a farm are flooded and used to harvest phosphorus over a period of years, then draining them, planting crops there, and submerging a different parcel. Ideally, the swampified land will also be rich in nutrients like the old Black Swamp soil back at the turn of the twentieth century.

This approach has proven so popular, and so full of potential, that at the time of this writing several groups are currently working on projects to rewild Northwest Ohio, including the EPA, H2Ohio, and the Black Swamp Conservancy. This is an exciting time for Lake Erie. To read these reports feels like we are on the cusp of something huge. While Toledo and Lake Erie were the first to capture global toxic algae attention in 2014, they have another opportunity to show everyone how to fix ecological disasters. The answer doesn't take chemicals, or expensive machines, or even a conflicted government's help—it just takes pragmatism, hard work, and common sense. Things Northwest Ohio has in abundance.

Having witnessed the impressive rewilding work back at the Evansport site does leave me with hope. But still, it's early in the process. What Lake Erie needs is nonecologists pitching in, too. It needs, I realize, people like me to get their hands dirty.

I reach out to Melanie Coulter and ask if there are any opportunities for me to get my hands dirty next time I am in Northwest Ohio.

26
THE CORNIEST MUSIC WE'VE EVER PLAYED

A while back I showed the song that I'd unearthed at the Hancock County Historical Society, the "Buckeye Traction Ditcher March," to the music director at my college, and we both cooked up a plan to have the university orchestra play it live.

It takes about a year, but eventually, Dr. Ben Bruflat and his student musicians are ready to perform the piece at the spring concert. The setting sun peeks through the long velvet curtains along the wall. Duke Hall is pretty full tonight. The band is sharp and focused, and they sound terrific. They perform pieces by celebrated composers Jacques Offenbach and Gustav Holst, as well as some modern video game scores that seem to energize the audience. These are huge, flowing, beautifully intricate pieces of art.

Toward the end of the evening, Bruflat steps to the microphone and announces, "This is without a doubt the corniest music we've ever played." He gives a good-natured chuckle and welcomes me onstage so I can tell the crowd more than they ever wanted to know about this odd twentieth-century jingle for mechanical drainage equipment.

I pack a lot of info about swamps, algae, and James B. Hill into a two-minute intro. But an important thing occurs to me while I stare out at the crowd: We are bringing this thing back from extinction. We are rewilding this song. "You are probably the first people to hear this piece of music in over one hundred years," I say. "I think that's pretty special. I hope you think so, too."

The song sounds like a cross between an oom-pah heavy polka and a John Philip Sousa march. It is, honestly, pretty corny. I don't exactly see how this peppy little number represents a giant machine clawing dirt from the earth and impregnating it with drainage tiles, and I'm curious whether it did, in fact, fill the factory's employees with pride about their jobs. The audience seems absolutely perplexed. No matter, because up near the front row, this bizarre moment in Northwest Ohio history brings me so much joy that it takes just about all my self-control not to squeal like a child riding a birthday pony.

Look at this: I have become the weird, sensitive, artistic person I always dreamed about. It's not the version I expected back in the 1990s, because that guy was going to release a number-one grunge album, punch Nazis in search of the Holy Grail, and marry Courtney Cox. But this version is still pretty cool. I'm proud. Not an easy thing to admit, when every instinct in my being tells me not to draw attention to myself. Instead, I've become even more proud of Northwest Ohio and the Great Black Swamp. I always loved Ohio, but this is different. I see now that my part of the world is absolutely unique, and uncelebrated.

Maybe pride is part of the solution?

In several places I have lived, civic pride is woven into daily life. Everyone in Portland seems to know a secret campsite on Mount

Hood, or the best Willamette Valley winery, or some favorite funky store off the main drag. Louisville residents are familiar with, if not experts on, bourbon, Muhammad Ali, and horse racing. In my current corner of Eastern Tennessee, folks wear Appalachian pride on their sleeve, celebrating the things that make this area a hardworking, big-hearted underdog. But Northwest Ohio?

Maybe that's the missing piece of the puzzle. We can have bills of rights or environmental groups doing great things like rewilding, but unless an area embraces this incredible yet weird, messy, muddy, wolf-ridden, crime-ridden, hope-filled history, it could all be for nothing. Being proud of this swamp legacy feels like the key to getting people to buy in to the cause and, eventually, eradicating toxic green algae on Lake Erie.

But that's tricky.

Often, rewilding grates against pride that already exists for the area. Take, for example, Curt Freese and Sean Gerrity, who once attempted to rewild the grassland plains of Northern Montana. This region was once home to herds of American bison. Like Ohio, its original landscape was completely transformed in less than a century. According to authors Paul Jepson and Cain Blythe in *Rewilding*, "Gerrity and Russell founded the American Prairie Reserve, a nonprofit organization with the audacious plan to buy ranches as they came on the market and restore herds parcel by parcel." Seems great. Nobody is getting hurt and we're bringing the land back to its natural state, right? "Not surprisingly their vision clashed with the cowboy frontier frames of independence, resilience, neighborly solidarity and ranching." Soon, the locals began fighting back. They did not like outsiders swooping in and telling them their way of life was wrong. The ranchers argued that reintroducing bison to the area would hurt their livelihood. "Save the cowboy: stop American Prairie Reserve" signs sprang up, and 133 landowners organized to prohibit bison on their collective properties. The Montana legislature passed a resolution asking the government to deny American Prairie Reserve permission to graze bison on state land.

Montana's locals successfully fought off rewilding efforts, but rewilding has had wins, too. In Argentina's Iberá Provincial Park in 1997, a land trust attempted to rewild ranch property in order to help bring back tapirs, giant anteaters, peccaries, and jaguars. "From the perspective of local ranchers, the idea of buying up land for no productive purpose made absolutely no sense," Jepson and Blythe write. Soon, rumors began spreading that the land trust was actually a CIA plot to control Argentina. It looked like Montana all over again. But the land trust took a different approach. They began using images and traditions of the local cowboy culture in their vision and communications. "The recovery of wildlife amplified and extended local people's sense of heritage and pride." It worked, and by 2018 the Iberá National Park had been created, combining the original 525,000-hectare provincial park and 140,000 additional hectares to create Argentina's largest natural preserve. That year, for the first time in seventy years, jaguar cubs were born in the area.

Unfortunately, my home currently sounds a lot more like Montana than Argentina. "Ohio has eliminated a large percentage of our natural wetlands," Sandusky County engineer Jim Moyer once said. "Well, I say good, because that's where I live."

"Ohio is much more anti-wetland than the rest of the Midwest," Christian Lenhart, co-owner of a farm near Defiance, told Sharon

Levy. "Talk to people about building a wetland in Defiance County, and they kind of think you're crazy. It goes beyond rationality. It's the communal memory of people dying of malaria in the Black Swamp."

These are dark thoughts, but that communal memory can be a positive thing, too. It could be something as simple as repositioning those thoughts. Some kind of regional Black Swamp Appreciation Day? Heck, I'd settle for a Simon Girty lookalike parade or a Bell Woods mosquito swatting contest.

Whatever it is, there's a feeling that our Great Black Swamp pride needs to come together quickly. While Northwest Ohio's rewilders quietly try to rescue its landscape, the rest of the country seems dead-set on driving off the ecological cliff. Take the Supreme Court's recent ruling on the case *Sackett v. EPA* (2023). This decision has all but doomed America's wetlands, essentially stripping the Clean Water Act of any of its remaining power to protect swamps. Justices Clarence Thomas and Neil Gorsuch went even further to disempower the Clean Water Act in their concurring opinions. According to the *University of Chicago Law Review*, "It is no exaggeration that, under [Thomas and Gorsuch's] view, the Clean Water Act would become a virtual nullity. The landmark 1972 Act that Congress enacted in the heyday of the nation's embrace of environmentalism would accomplish little more than the several Rivers and Harbors Acts that Congress passed during the 1890s." Neil Gorsuch, not surprisingly, is the son of Anne Gorsuch. What are the odds that the vision of destruction started by a Supreme Court justice's mother would be finished by her son nearly forty years later? That's the negative side of communal memory.

27
THE CAT IS OUT OF THE BAG

I have a Google alert set up for news about toxic algae, and lately, it's always going off.

> Lake Superior, once thought to be impervious to algae thanks to its pristine waters, has seen its first HABs.
>
> The University of Miami claimed to have found a link between HABs and Alzheimer's-like deterioration in dolphin brains.
>
> CNN reported on sea lions and dolphins washing ashore in California, saying as many as sixty reports an hour were coming in. John Warner of the Marine Mammal Care Center described it as "the ocean coughing up death."
>
> HAB were reported in Utah, Idaho, and Arkansas.

I don't have the space to keep going, but I could.

A global HAB study found the number of blooms was on the rise in the US Gulf Coast, the Caribbean, Central America, South America, northern Asia, northern Europe, and the Mediterranean. According to one writer, "That data set includes more than 9,500 instances since 1985 where blooms closed beaches, killed fish, or poisoned people and shellfish." Citing the same study, *Scientific American* noted, "Intensifying aquaculture in places like Finland, China, Algeria, Argentina and Russia could also be helping to intensify algae blooms in those regions."

I've asked several brilliant scientific minds "What does success look like?" and "When will we see changes?" The answers tend to be noncommittal. Nobody seems to want to plant a flag and guess what the future of toxic algae looks like, probably because the odds feel more and more unwinnable every day.

Multiple people I speak to, though, recommend one person for the best glimpse into the future.

NOAA's Dr. Reagan Errera and her team are the vanguard of HAB research. She is likely the closest thing toxic algae has to an oracle. When I contacted her, she invited me up to Lake Erie to see their super-high-tech remote-controlled aquatic drone, the Environmental Sample Processor (ESP), which she calls a "lab in a can." Unfortunately, the ESP was struck by a boat the Saturday night before I arrived and was pretty much destroyed. Errera welcomed me to NOAA's Ann Arbor, Michigan headquarters as a consolation prize.

The National Oceanographic and Atmospheric Administration is a massive government organization that is tasked with everything from forecasting weather to monitoring oceanic and atmospheric conditions, charting the seas, conducting deep-sea exploration, and even managing fishing and protection of some endangered species. "We're not sexy like the weather service," one employee told *The New Republic*. "We can't tell you when a tornado is going to hit or if a hurricane is gonna be a Category 3. Our job is to not be seen and not be heard, and keep everybody safe." Nowhere is that more obvious than NOAA's Great Lakes Environmental Research Laboratory.

On a bright, crisp August morning, almost exactly one decade to the day since the 2014 toxic algae crisis, I find the single-story building tucked neatly in an office park on the opposite side of town from the hustle and bustle of the University of Michigan. Errera, curly-haired and wearing jeans and running sneakers, greets me with the upbeat enthusiasm I have come to expect in my ecological experts. Despite grim news, scientists all seem like a chipper bunch. It's hard not to get onboard when you are around them. I am immediately given a tour of the grounds, with its very clean and impressive laboratories and workshops, including one featuring the guts of the destroyed Lab in a Can. We spend a moment mourning the heart of the technology: a clear plastic cylinder, about the size of a duffel bag, which houses a series of wires, circuitry, and tiny test tubes. The machine can take samples of Lake Erie's water and process it in less than an hour, giving nearly instantaneous data to Errera's team. This is a huge leap forward in their ability to warn people about hazardous lake conditions. The ESP will eventually get fixed, but it'll take some time, which is a shame because it's peak toxic algae season right now.

Errera has dedicated her life to HABs. She is a research ecologist with NOAA's Great Lakes Research Laboratory, a former professor at Louisiana State University, and the author of a popular TED Talk on the wonders of phytoplankton. She discovered her life's work while studying in Australia, where she first became exposed to HABs. "Algae is kind of an underdog, right?" she tells me. "They shouldn't be hurting the ecosystem, but they are, and that's kind of where my interest took off."

Some of the technology here is so advanced I am forbidden to take photos. But one thing I am allowed to snap pictures of is a refrigerator filled with glass beakers. Each container is tightly covered with aluminum foil and looks like the grossest collection of leftovers you've ever seen. "I have to remember who's toxic and who's not," Errera says. Some of the containers are that familiar kale shake green, while others are completely clear, some are speckled with green bits, and one looks as if someone hacked a snotty phlegm wad into some clean tap water. Errera pulls several beakers out to show me.

Like Melanie Coulter talking about baby trees, Errera personifies her subjects. "Okay, so he's pretty toxic. The most toxic guy that we have is this guy, who's not doing that well in there."

I'm surprised to learn that the color and density of algae does not necessarily corelate to toxicity. Some of the crystal-clear samples are the deadliest, while many of the ugliest, like that ball of boogers, are harmless. It speaks to the difficulty of NOAA's job with Lake Erie. It also makes me wonder what happened to the windsurfer dude in Toledo who said only pea soup algae is dangerous.

Back in Errera's office, we chat about algae and the Lab in a Can and the coincidence that our kids are exactly the same age. Eventually, we end up discussing some of the potential uses of toxic algae. "I know the Department of Energy has looked into taking different types of phytoplankton and using that as an energy source."

I laugh and tell her about the Army Corps' failed yoga mat plan. "I could see a day where they are just harvesting HABs," I laugh. "Scooping it up with one of those bucket planes like they use for forest fires."

"An interesting side note, the US Forest Service is worried about the firefighters because they're going in and picking up the water that has cyanobacteria, putting it on a forest fire, and that just combusts all the toxin right away," she says. "If you pour them on the fire, the cells are going to bust open, releasing that toxin into the air."

"Oh, god. Like airborne toxic algae?" I am reminded of just about every time anyone tried to do something useful and good in the Great Black Swamp, how it has always seemed to backfire in one way or another. Glenn Colerider would make a meal out of this news.

The conversation eventually works itself around to a point where I ask about whether she wants to predict the future of toxic algae on Lake Erie.

"For cyanobacteria, I'm going to be a little doom and gloom," she says. "It doesn't look good. The planet is changing, and our climate is changing in a way that's going to promote them more."

"I've gone around and talked to tons of different people, and nobody seems to have a clear idea about this," I say. "But what I'm wondering is, what can be done about HABs?"

"Yeah, the cat's out of the bag. And, yeah, it's going to take a while to," she pauses, "not solve, but hopefully alleviate the problem."

I ask: If she had a magic wand she could wave over the lake, what would it be?

"I guess the biggest magic wand that I would wave is educating the public more. There are people out there that don't know why it's green. They're just like, oh, Lake Erie is always green. I wish that we could reach more people and really let them know where you can be and where you can't be, or what kind of decisions you need to make during your recreational time."

I am, again, reminded of that confident windsurfer in Toledo. And Les and Pam, and the woman working the desk at the National Museum of the Great Lakes, and frankly, everyone I talked to in Toledo. I wish there was a little Dr. Reagan Errera hologram that popped up in everyone's house and shared this kind of information.

But the Lab in a Can is nowhere near that advanced. And despite the fact that all this valuable information is out there, it seems like the bulk of the population continues to choose to carry on like nothing abnormal is happening. It makes me wonder, what makes our brains do things like that?

28
WE'RE ALL KINGS HERE

I'm barreling down the interstate, about an hour south of Ann Arbor now. It's sunny, and the highway is crowded with families squeezing in one last quick vacation before school starts. Bowling Green is just off Exit 181, and I see the Jerome Library sprouting up above the football stadium and the dorms and full green trees. There's a small urge to pop in just to check in on my old friend Glenn Colerider and rewatch that grainy VHS tape of *The Story of the Great Black Swamp*. But this is not one of those lazy drives where I can stop and visit. This is a runaway train to Tennessee, because classes begin in a couple days and I've done almost no course prep this summer. I have been putting off writing syllabi in favor of toxic green algae and corn and labs in cans and starting my life over again.

I keep kicking around Reagan Ererra's magic wand idea. One of the brightest minds in the world of toxic algae simply wants the public to be more educated, to pay more attention to their land, to acknowledge that this place is flawed, and love it for those flaws. But instead, we do what we've always done when things get difficult or weird.

I've asked a few psychology professor friends why the Northwest Ohio mind behaves this way, but they didn't really have any answers. I asked my therapist, and she didn't know either. I always ask in regards to toxic algae, but secretly, I'm also thinking about me and my failed marriage. Stuck for answers and filled with anxiety thanks to I-75's notoriously intense love of speeding semitrucks that box you in, I play the audiobook version of Jon Lauck's *The Good Country: A History of the American Midwest 1800–1900*. Expectations are low. I bought this book in the hopes Lauck might mention anything about the Great Black Swamp or Northwest Ohio, but considering his work focuses on all twelve states that make up the Midwest, I doubt he'll spend much time in my homeland.

Then, magic strikes as the billboards and green farm fields blur past my window. Lauck's maximalist vision of the Midwest hooks me before I even reach the Lima city limits.

Lima, a modest industrial city of thirty-five thousand residents, is the southernmost border of the Great Black Swamp. It was named in honor of the Peruvian capital, where its shipments of quinine, one of the few known cures for malaria in those mosquitos-aplenty early settlement days, came from in the 1800s. This gritty white powder was so crucial that it was often found on every dinner table beside the salt. Pioneers would gulp down a knife blade's worth every morning in hopes of warding off the disease.

Lauck quotes one orator from the nineteenth century, probably about the time Lima was welcoming in those shipments: "Ohio was the truest democracy that had yet existed."

Is it too soon to say Jon Lauck is my favorite writer of all time? Probably, but I can't help myself. His book repeatedly holds the

Buckeye State up on quite a pedestal. This is not something I'm used to hearing in a world filled with Bill Bryson, and Charles Dickens, and my college friends who talked so much trash about my homeland. I'm only a little ways into the book, but I decide that if called upon, I will someday take a bullet for Jon Lauck.

Lauck credits Ohio as really being the first state established in the western territories, so it was the first to do a lot of things, and its political progressiveness often did them better than established coastal states. Among a host of other cool distinctions, Ohio was staunchly antislavery, pro-literacy, and pro-college before just about any other American state. Most interesting is that Ohio had a badass egalitarian streak I never knew about.

In the early years of America, the East Coast states were still rooted in the English way of doing things, especially with their strict class system. Meanwhile, the South was locked into the aristocratic fiefdoms of plantation life. Both left shockingly little room for a middle class and for average folks to become educated, earn a living wage, and govern themselves. Ohio, therefore, was a true experiment. "Out in the Midwest, people could be uniquely free. A condition they widely recognized and routinely celebrated," Lauck writes. "Ohio was founded [as] a nearly true democratic community and absent of feudal spirit."

I hit a little bit of traffic in Dayton, the city where my ex-wife and I met in college. Here, *The Good Country* notes, in 1837, Ohio Judge Timothy Walker said that because the Northwest Ordinance set forth the principles of a democratic society from the beginning, no ancient rubbish had to be cleared away. No longer were people beholden to either the repressive ways of Eastern or Southern life. About the time

I hit Cincinnati's city limits, I laugh at this chapter in the book. This must be the first and last time Ohio was ever considered edgy.

The idealistic, youthful state took this new responsibility seriously. Lauck says, "When young Louis Phillipe, later to be king of France, visited Ohio, a straight-shooting tavern owner told him that he had many royals at his establishment. 'Who were they?' asked the young Duke. 'We're all kings here,' declared the proud Buckeye before he kicked the future king out for complaining."

Crossing over the murky Ohio River as the sun begins to set, it occurs to me that Lauck's insight is exactly what I've needed.

Here is the answer that's kept me scavenging around Northwest Ohio. Why are we so fixated on being normal? I have ample time to ponder while sitting in a traffic jam. (Rush hour in Cincinnati rivals any cosmopolitan destination two or three times its size. I've tried to coin the phrase "Cincinnati is the Los Angeles of the Midwest...for traffic." But it hasn't caught on, sadly.) What I gather is that this fixation on normalcy is rooted in Ohio's early existence as an experimental community. Dare I say, Ohio's punk era? I'm reminded of how Kurt Cobain taught me about K Records and punk rock ethics of equality and the anyone-can-do-it spirit.

Is Jon Lauck's book the Come as You Are *for my forties?* I wonder. It very well could be, and I'm ready for it.

America's powers-that-be were testing out whether normal folks could actually govern themselves. Ohio went to great lengths to prove that people who were not from wealthy, landholding means could create the ideal America. Maybe farmers and laborers and schoolteachers could even make a *better* America. Since they didn't have money or power, this fringe state knew it had to work hard to create stability. Normalcy. That meant honoring different opinions and avoiding outright derision, no matter how heated, difficult, or weird things got. Being even-keeled was a necessary survival instinct if Ohio were to grow and thrive.

I see it today. This spirit is deeply embedded in everyone I spoke to, and it's in me. But today's version is not the same as what Lauck's book talks about. This democratic idealism was maybe once a conscious effort at egalitarianism, but it has mutated into extreme ambivalence. What started off as a one-for-all, all-for-one spirit slowly evolved into a smile, a shrug, and back to normal.

This shirking of attention was not a defense mechanism but rather a tool to make all voices equal. Was that always successful? Of course not. But I'm starting to realize this state of mind is a lot more impressive than I ever could have imagined, even though, in Lake Erie's case, it came at a steep price.

"This common midwestern culture blended the conventions of Christianity; a midwesternized Victorian ethos of self-improvement, self-help, and striving; free labor, anti-slavery ideology; a reverence for physical work; the bourgeois views on prudence and temperance; and educational aspiration, optimism, democratic openness, republicanism, and meritocracy together to create productive citizens and a region of uplift and ambition," writes Lauck. "The result was a society where Christianity, republican law and order, market culture, civic obligation and a midwestern-modified gentility of manner largely prevailed."

Rolling deep into Kentucky, I feel this description like a dart plucking into my chest. Despite my artiness and weirdness, I am drawn to this type of Midwestern mentality. Finally free of the bumper-to-bumper traffic, another thought hits me: Was I always searching for this type of stable, normal Midwestern life? My ex was a Kentuckian, a Southerner, which never seemed like such a big difference before. But now, it makes me wonder if that personality difference doomed us from the start. My instincts always said to fight those Midwestern tendencies, to be some unique little unicorn, but I have always had the urge to return home, physically and mentally. I'm no unicorn; I'm a salmon. There's a radar in my heart, leading me back to the comforts of my Northwest Ohio and its mindset, even as I see its flaws so clearly. That was something my ex-wife and I did not share. How could she? *Why* would she? It's like this frame of mind was just as toxic to her as it was to me. We were like two inert elements that were completely harmless, maybe even beneficial, on our own—but when we combined we were phosphorus and lake water.

In Jon Lauck, I have finally found someone who understands me and my people. He is able to look under the hood of the Northwest Ohio brain and see things I never saw before. I didn't need a psychologist or an ecologist to tell me why Northwest Ohioans act this way—I needed a historian.

Long after dark, I roll into my Tennessee home filled with Ohio pride, and it occurs to me that I'm still no closer than I was this morning to knowing what the future holds for Lake Erie.

29

BEGINNING AGAIN

Bowling Green's *Sentinel-Tribune* does not list its circulation numbers, and it does not appear on *Muck Rack*'s list of the top thirty Ohio periodicals by circulation size, which means it's even smaller than a paper called *The Rural-Urban Record*. And most likely, that means it's one of the smallest newspapers in print anywhere. It's the world's loss, if you ask me, because today this mighty little paper has the scoop of the century: "BGSU Research Finds Reduced Levels of Harmful Algae Toxins in Sandusky Bay."

The article features a photo of young grad students standing on a boat painted in blisteringly vivid BGSU Orange (the school has its own Pantone: PMS 166 C), hauling up water samples. The story interviews the professor in charge of the research, George Bullerjahn, a name I recognize because he patiently answered some questions a few years earlier. He was the guy who told me to "thank some cyanobacteria."

It's the first positive news I've ever read about Lake Erie's toxic algae that deals with solid scientific evidence and not the limitless potential of Army Corps yoga mats. I'm so excited that I can't bring myself to finish the article. This happens when I'm confronted with really good or really bad news. My brain gets overloaded by the emotional swing, and it has to slowly peck away at the words. For example, it took about four breaks to joyously read my final divorce paperwork.

According to the article, a small inlet on Lake Erie, about forty miles east of Toledo, used to be teeming with toxic water warnings and green algae, but over the last several years has experienced a sharp decrease in toxicity. Such a drop that, according to WHO standards, one could actually drink this water now. Sure, nobody's throwing a parade about the water not being deadly, but still, this is the first tangible victory in a decade-long attempt to reclaim the Great Black Swamp.

There's a weird elation, mixed with surprise. I dash off a quick email to Bullerjahn, asking if he remembers me asking a bunch of boneheaded questions back when I was a mere baby in the toxic algae world. A week later, we are staring at one another on a Zoom call through our computers.

"How did it feel when you started getting these results?"

"It's fantastic. I mean, we weren't expecting this at all," says Bullerjahn from his Bowling Green office. His shelves are delightfully crammed with books and scientific journals. He's wearing a checked shirt and has tousled gray hair, and he speaks with that same infectious enthusiasm for microcystin and algae that I keep encountering throughout the scientific community.

It's easy to match his enthusiasm from my office in Tennessee, though I am nervously trying to position my head in a way that blocks the wall behind me. I have one of those '80s library posters proclaiming "READ" in bold letters. I'm embarrassed because it's a giant, campy photo of British songwriter Sting, wearing a frilly white shirt, sitting before a castle, dramatically holding a copy of *Frankenstein*.

Bullerjahn tells me the toxicity of Sandusky Bay has been decreasing for five years straight, ever since the city removed a dam upstream to try and bring back the fish population. "They're actually seeing sturgeon spawning upstream," he says. "Any way you can get rid of water stagnation is going to improve things." He is extremely proud of his team of grad students, doctoral candidates, and researchers. They recently published their findings in what is now my all-time favorite magazine: *Harmful Algae*.

Here is the thing people have been hoping for. We want to see water quality improve, to see a greater harmony between agriculture and the ecosystem. I want to see people taking pride in our Northwest Ohio. Granted, one small bay that feeds into Lake Erie is not a sign that our troubles are over. But it's a sign that something is changing, and changing for the better. Maybe this is a sign that the lake has begun again?

I ask Bullerjahn what he sees in the future, and he is a beam of sunlight for someone who has been paddling down the rivers of Hades for so long. To hear him tell it, we are holding something rare in our hands: hope.

He tells me that the 2104 Toledo algae bloom "was an isolated incident. We know why and how it happened, and we know how to correct things. I don't worry about human exposure there. No one's going to die," he says. "I'm optimistic because water treatment plants are doing a very good job of protecting us."

Maybe this is what it felt like to see the Clean Water Act start to transform the water in the '70s? I ask Bullerjahn if he thinks Nixon's begrudging life preserver to the environment could work as a guide.

"We can do it again. You know, the will is there. We saw that if we know what to do, we can actually get there and do it now," he says. He suggests we focus on not only phosphorus but also nitrogen. He calls it *dual nutrient management*. "Phosphorus alone won't do it. Okay? Microcystis is a very good scavenger of phosphorus, and it needs nitrogen."

It will hit me later that I, too, have changed for the better. I'm no longer nervous to be around such brilliant scientific minds. I no longer cover up my anxiety with dumb jokes like I did on my walk through Bell Woods with Melanie Coulter. I'm happy to admit when I'm in the dark so that these experts can teach me. And I'm still a little amazed when I realize I can actually keep my head above water during these chats.

"It seems to speak again to the complexity of all this. There's, unfortunately, not just one switch we flip and fix everything," I say, so engrossed that I've forgotten about Sting peeking over my shoulder. "You remove the dam, and it helps a little bit. You put back in some wetlands, and it helps a little bit. You start working alongside the farmers, and that helps a bit. And it all starts to add up, right? When things start working together you get what's happening in Sandusky Bay."

"I completely agree, yeah," he says.

I want to call the professor who gave me a C back in that college biology class. I suddenly feel like the smartest man in the world. Is this what it takes? To be proud of ourselves and our home, and to want to make an impact, to want to understand the inner workings of it all? Like Reagan Errera says, to educate the public? Not just be educated, though, but to use that to make a change?

While I might think the Sandusky Bay news is the first wave of a revolution, I get the impression Bullerjahn sees things a little more long term. He's more patient than I am.

"We'll never completely get rid of the blooms," he says. "We're going to need to change land use parameters for agriculture, where we will have to take some land out of production completely, identifying so-called hot spots, which are nutrient-rich and releasing nutrients. It's going to take a decade or more, but I think land use decisions will be made either by individuals or by the government."

It's hard to think like that. In another decade it'll have been twenty years since the 2014 algae crisis. It's incredible that three days of the worst toxic algae imaginable could take that long to heal. But I suppose when the alternative is to leave things be and let them get worse, it doesn't feel so long.

Elated by his optimism and vision, I go back to the *Sentinel-Tribune* article that inspired this conversation. I overlooked it before, but the reporter takes time to interview a few of the students, those people who will be guiding the change in the next decade on Lake Erie.

One person interviewed, Kate Brown, is studying for a doctorate in biology and chose BGSU specifically because it has a strong water quality and cyanobacteria program. "It has been really impressive seeing the residents around Sandusky Bay being so involved in their body of water," Brown says in the story. "They are passionate about the water quality and wanting to fix it."

Maybe the Great Black Swamp will be the next Iberá National Park in Argentina? This next generation sees that a rewilding campaign isn't just about ecology—it's about instilling pride in people. It feels like the next generation that Bullerjahn and others are fostering will eventually yield positive results. You never know what's going to be the tipping point.

PART V

When we love the Earth,

we are able to love ourselves more fully.

—bell hooks

30
ELON MUSK'S CHAINSAW

Some months later, a harsh lesson in tipping points hits close to home. I am reminded that points can tip in the direction I predict and hope, but they can also tip wildly away from those hopes.

"We're cutting down the size of government," President Donald Trump said early in his second presidency. "We're bloated. We're sloppy." In order to fix this perceived problem during the first months of 2025, he tasked the world's richest man, billionaire Elon Musk, to run the recently created Department of Government Efficiency (DOGE). On the surface, DOGE's goal was to seek out and eliminate wasteful spending in the government, but Musk and a small team quickly began gutting thousands of jobs throughout all levels of federal agencies. Public outcry came swiftly after seemingly benign organizations like Veterans Affairs, the National Park Service, and Health and Human Services were hollowed out.

Musk appeared to take on the role of villain and agitator with particular glee, once, early in his tenure, jumping onstage at the

Conservative Political Action Conference with a large smile, wearing a black hat, sunglasses, and a black jacket and wielding a bright red chainsaw. Right-wing Argentine President Javier Milei (a man the *Journal of Democracy* once called "impolite, foul-mouthed, and colorful") had just given Musk the saw, which was inscribed with Milei's slogan: "Viva la libertad, carajo." According to the *Associated Press*, this is Spanish for "Long live liberty, damn it."

The implication was that Musk now had the power to chop up the government as he saw fit.

With that, a sort of chainsaw fever spread across Washington in the opening one hundred days of Trump's presidency. It seemed as if the president was willfully disregarding all political norms and traditions of the past, even ones he had previously honored. For instance, there seemed to be a preference for picking nonbureaucrats to lead federal agencies, such as vaccination-denier Robert Kennedy Jr. being put in charge of the now-beleaguered United States Department of Health and Human Services, or WWE's Linda McMahon being tasked to lead—and admittedly dismantle—the Department of Education, or the choice of Fox News personality Pete Hegseth to be thrust into the role of secretary of defense.

Nowhere did these cuts capture my attention more than with the EPA and NOAA.

EPA Administrator Lee Zeldin, someone, surprisingly, with a political background, immediately jumped on the DOGE bandwagon and mirrored Ronald Reagan and Anne Gorsuch's leadership decisions of nearly five decades earlier. Zeldin claimed he would disembowel his own agency's budget by 65 percent, which meant potentially cutting around ten thousand jobs, eliminating an estimated $1 billion in grants, and launching the biggest deregulatory action in American history, which, according to the EPA's website, included everything from reevaluating limits set on the oil and gas industry to loosening mercury and air toxics standards for coal-fired power plants and easing up on wastewater restrictions across the board. "We don't need to be spending all that money that went through the EPA last year," Zeldin told Fox News. "We don't want it. We don't need it."

The shockwaves of job loss and environmental concern set off alarm bells around the country.

"The feeling has been 'you've got to be kidding me,'" one EPA staffer told *The Guardian*. California Congressional Representative Zoe Lofgren claimed that Trump and Musk "are putting their polluter buddies' bottom lines over the health and safety of Americans."

With the EPA getting dissected, it was only a matter of time until NOAA, too, became the target of Musk's chainsaw. According to *Time*, "The current cuts to NOAA were equal parts ill-timed and foreseeable. Project 2025, the conservative manifesto whose policies are increasingly being adopted by the Trump Administration, includes a section on page 674 of the 900-plus page document headed 'Break Up NOAA.' On the next page the agency is described as 'one of the main drivers of the climate change alarm industry.'" Project 2025, it should be noted, was created by the Heritage Foundation—the same group that gave Ronald Reagan the advice to virtually eliminate the EPA back in 1980.

The National Oceanic and Atmospheric Administration felt an immediate blow as DOGE claimed it would be eliminating 10 percent of its thirteen-thousand-person staff nationwide. This included serious cuts at NOAA's Ann Arbor outpost, the Great Lakes Environmental Research Laboratory (GLERL).

Dr. Bret Collier, who led the Ecosystem Dynamics branch at the lab, was let go amid the 2025 cuts, and he told *The New Republic* that he had never been contacted to ask what his team did, about the risks that might be posed by axing them, or whether doing so would endanger programs mandated by federal legislation. The staffing cuts, instead, seemed to come completely out of the dark.

"It was a little devastating," Dr. Reagan Errera told me over the phone, a month after DOGE's first cuts to her office. "The day before, we had a retirement party for our lab director. It was a huge celebration, and we're all happy that she had such a vibrant career. Employees from twenty years ago came into town, and then the following day, we were going about business as usual, and about three o'clock in the afternoon, the emails started rolling. No one was prepared. We went from a super high to a devastating low. So that was Thursday. Friday, it was like walking into a funeral."

According to the *Toledo Blade*, the cuts included at least fifteen employees in NOAA's already lean laboratory in Ann Arbor. To Errera, the cuts were especially personal, because among those who unexpectedly lost their job was her husband—Dr. Bret Collier.

"When you remove a staffer," Collier told *The New Republic*'s Kate Aronoff in her article "Elon Musk's DOGE Cuts Could Kill Your Dog," "there's not another staffer that can just pick up that work. I don't want to say we don't have a deep bench. There's no bench. We're one deep everywhere....If we can't do our job, you can't drink the water."

"I think it was a lazy approach," Rick Spinrad, who served as NOAA administrator until Trump came into office, told *Fast Company*.

With this in mind, NOAA's Lake Erie office discovered it suddenly had to make some tough decisions. For instance, Errera said they must now pick and choose how to deploy their workforce, knowing that either choice will result in danger for Americans in and around the Great Lakes. Where once NOAA had funding to both put things like the Lab in a Can out in the water to report current algae conditions (R.I.P. original Lab in a Can; Errera says they no longer have the money to repair it) and pay to repair their fleet of boats, now, they worry they have to pick one or the other. This means they might have to sacrifice those real-time toxin analysis maps that I used in Toledo, which, more importantly, warn water managers that toxins in the area are spiking. "So those are the types of questions that we have to ask: where do we put all our effort, because we are now a reduced workforce." This means that communities, like Toledo, that depend on NOAA's data to help safely manage their drinking water supplies could be more vulnerable because of the DOGE cuts. It feels like we could see a 2014 water crisis all over again.

"The work conducted at GLERL is critical to the health and preservation of the Great Lakes," the *Toledo Blade* pointed out. "The loss of experienced scientists, researchers, and support staff at GLERL threatens to undermine the effectiveness of ongoing studies and disrupt critical work that supports regional environmental management and policy decisions."

On a national level, the agency is responsible for so many other day-to-day things it makes one's head spin. NOAA's work "isn't a 'nice' thing to have—this is an absolute essential for aviation," Rick Spinrad told *Fast Company*. "I would argue that NOAA's weather information is as important as jet fuel to the aviation industry. You can't fly without it." In addition, shipping lanes could be affected by the potential loss of NOAA's forecasts, and according to Great Lakes Fisheries, the fishing industry, which has an annual value of $7 billion and supports seventy-five thousand jobs, could be in jeopardy. *Fast Company* also pointed out that the agency also tracks space-related issues, like solar flares and geomagnetic storms, which can disrupt GPS navigation and communication systems. "If you're flying from San Francisco to New York, if there's a solar storm and it may impact GPS, your flight may be redirected to the south," Spinrad said. "There are literally hundreds of NOAA weather service employees who are involved in providing that information to the FAA. This is not just when there's a storm. This is all the time, 24/7/365."

"It will be unfortunate," the editors of the *Toledo Blade* wrote, "if slashing NOAA for short-term gains ends up with long-term costs in terms of algae growth, threats to the water supply, and invasive species." The paper also pointed out, in a different article, "Substantial cuts in NOAA's budget won't necessarily eliminate forecasts for and tracking of harmful algal blooms. The public will, hopefully, continue to get those, as well as hurricane forecasts and tracking by the National Hurricane Center, plus severe weather forecasts and monitoring by the National Weather Service."

After the initial wave of public surprise, the Trump administration and DOGE did not seem discouraged from continuing to use their chainsaw. Instead, it seems that this chaos was part of the plan. This would just be, as Aronoff wrote in *The New Republic*, "clearing the way for private companies like AccuWeather to snap up lucrative new government contracts for work that has long been considered a public service." However, experts say this type of transition could take years and set back current successfully operating systems indefinitely. In addition, there are concerns about whether for-profit companies can be trusted to run systems that the public depends on for its safety, whether it be on the land, on the water, or in the air.

"If NOAA gets broken up and privatized...the threats to aviation safety will increase dramatically," Jeff Masters, cofounder of commercial weather-prediction site Weather Underground, told *Fast Company*. "The years-long transition period to a system where private companies do aviation forecasting would bring chaotic and unpredictable consequences to a system that needs utmost stability. 'If it ain't broke, don't fix it!' definitely applies here."

The aftermath of Musk's chainsaw has left stakeholders reeling and fearing that this is only the beginning of far steeper cuts. There seems to be a feeling among the scientific and environmental communities that this is far worse, and far more confusing, than anyone ever would have guessed.

"These cuts were misguided, ill-informed, and consequential," Spinrad said.

"It's an absolute joke," one NOAA staffer told *The Guardian*.

"Dysfunction is the polite way of putting it, you could also say it is incompetent chaos," said Andrew Rosenberg, formerly the deputy director of NOAA's national marine fisheries service, said in that same article.

Worse, all this pain and suffering and uncertainty could all be for no financial gain to taxpayers. "Slashing NOAA's staffing and budget will do precious little to achieve the ostensible goal of the White House," said *Time*. "Eliminate NOAA's entire 13,000-person staff and you have cut just 0.43% of the federal government's three million-strong workforce....NOAA's $6.6 billion annual budget represents just 0.097% of the $6.75 trillion Washington spent in fiscal year 2024."

At such an early stage, it's impossible to know how all this will play out, and the future for NOAA, the EPA, and other agencies is almost certain to keep evolving beyond this book's publication. But for those whose careers and livelihoods depend on these things, it is a scary time. You can't put a tree back together once it's been chainsawed. Perhaps encapsulating this strange moment best, *The Guardian*'s Oliver Milman wrote: "A sense of chaos has gripped [NOAA... with key staff hastily fired and then rehired, cuts to vital weather forecasting operations and even a new, unsecured server that led to staff being deluged by obscene spam emails," he said. "That staff got dozens of spam-like emails in January, one of them with a lewd title about the president and another stating: 'The next 4 years has an [*sic*] 99% chance of shit showers.'"

31
THE BOWL

Amid the growing shitstorm of political, bureaucratic, and environmental upheaval, it comes as no shock that the tone of everyday life in my former home feels pretty steady. Northwest Ohio has a way of taking bad times and making the best of them. We've done it before. This place was a deadly swamp, this place was killing off people with malaria, this place was once America's Dead Sea, this place once threatened to blow John Denver up with a grenade because he laughed at us. And in every instance, we kept our head down, did the work, and created the new normal. There's a curiosity in me that wonders if that kind of new normal is exactly what's needed to ride out this turbulence. I see now that that mentality is not just a weakness but also a strength. But strength like that moves slowly.

Change is hard work, but luckily, this is a place that doesn't know any other way to operate than by hard work. We were so hardworking, in fact, that when I was in school there was no such thing as spring break. It wasn't until I was in college that I discovered this was not just some phony holiday on episodes of *Saved by the Bell* but a real thing where students and teachers took a week off to have a vacation—right in the middle of all that hard work.

So, it's not surprising that now that I'm a teacher, I spend my spring break working. I am, frankly, pretty thrilled by the prospect of hard work over this year's break because Melanie Coulter has taken me up on my request to get my hands dirty in the Great Black Swamp. I just didn't realize there would be a dress code.

According to Melanie's email: "Wear tall muck boots. There will be mud and standing water to walk through. Bring leather work gloves. We'll be dealing with metal sheeting as part of the herp camera trap. Also bring water and a sack lunch. There are no facilities out there, so just be prepared for that."

"Muck boots?" I wonder, recalling how I ruined my tennis shoes last time she took me on a Black Swamp adventure. I will not make that mistake twice. I like to think I learn my lessons once in a while and have certainly learned so many lessons since then, both about the Great Black Swamp and toxic algae and about myself.

Melanie concludes: "We'll show you the largest remnant of the Great Black Swamp in our preserve system."

››››››

A week later I am back in Ohio and pulling into a small gravel parking lot beside Forrest Woods Nature Preserve. It's about thirty minutes outside of the nearest city, Defiance, and that's only if you define cities based on whether or not they have a small college and a

Buffalo Wild Wings. Melanie and land steward Charlotte Rice pull up in a heavy-duty maroon Ford F-150. We say hello and all pile in together, creeping down the single-lane asphalt road, looking for the head of a very poorly marked trail.

I chuckle, because it seems like every time Melanie and I go somewhere we can't find the trail entrances. Either I am bad luck or she is the keeper of secret places here in Northwest Ohio. Eventually, we find it and step across a flimsy chain blocking ATV traffic. "Down this path," Melanie says, pointing at a thin straightaway, glowing black with stagnant water and dead leaves, "is The Bowl."

I feel invincible in these tall black rubber boots. I was hoping for a cool pair with an octopus pattern, but the Walmart in my rural part of Tennessee did not oblige me. It's one of those early spring days when ice was on my windshield in the morning, but now the sun is so warm I strip down to a sweatshirt. Birds trill above us, and the bare tree branches sway like skeletons.

For ten minutes our boots work through dark water and pull to the surface with a sound like ripping Velcro. Around a bend we reach our destination. For thousands of years, the nearby Maumee River and DeLarme Creek have been flooding and receding, ebbing and flowing, seasons in and seasons out, gently changing this forty-acre patch of land. The result of all this expansion and contraction is "The Bowl," a twenty-foot-deep crater about the size of a football field.

For a moment, the birds and breeze vanish in my ear. My attention is drawn to something I assumed I'd never see. It's like the heart of this crater has come directly out of my imagination. Like something Glenn Colerider would have described in that cheerful grandpa voice.

Here is the Great Black Swamp.

The Bowl is a stretch of dark water and slime. Its calm surface reflects the winter trees and blue sky and white clouds. "Is this what it would have looked like back then?"

I have asked this question so many times that I kind of don't even cringe anymore. It's become just the thing I say before someone disappoints me.

"Pretty much," Melanie says. "This is what it looked like, yeah."

I am momentarily stunned.

"The tree cover isn't as dense as it would have been, since the ash and elm trees have all died. But, yeah, this is as close to the real thing as we can get."

We inch down The Bowl's sloping sides and stand on the grainy knuckles of an oak tree's roots near the center of the crater. I am hovering over the still, dark water while Melanie turns over rocks and decayed sticks, hoping to show me a red salamander.

I can picture my great-great-great-grandfather, who probably looked like me, probably had a soft Dutch accent, and probably hired a man with a Buckeye Traction Ditcher to roar through his 159 acres that once probably looked about like this. I'm sad he did that, considering how much pollution it eventually contributed, but also grateful because of everything that ditch has given me.

Melanie and Charlotte don't have any luck tracking down the salamander. "Should we go build the herp trap?" Melanie asks and starts walking back toward the truck.

"Yes," I say, still unclear what a herp trap is. Too proud to ask.

Was Henry Wensink this proud? Did he not know what he was getting into, moving to the malaria capital of the world, dreaming of planting corn? Is this just the latest in a long line of Wensinks getting into messes because they don't bother to ask questions?

I am reminded of my marriage, seeing the problems but not being brave enough to ask questions.

Back in the truck, Charlotte at the wheel, we drive to another site a few miles away. I finally build up the nerve. "So, remind me, what exactly will we be doing?"

"We're setting up a herp trap."

"So, we are trapping something? Like an animal?" We reach our destination and hop out.

Charlotte flips down the heavy tailgate with a thump. We drag out a wheelbarrow, a shovel, and a pickax.

"No, just taking pictures. Basically, we are setting up a fence that redirects salamanders to pass under a motion-sensor camera."

"So, you're counting salamanders?"

"Right."

We unload a dozen lengths of iron rebar and a fifty-foot roll of black aluminum. We carefully guide the fully stocked wheelbarrow down a badly rutted trail, nearly spilling our careful pile of supplies more than a few times.

I was hoping to plant trees or rip apart drainage tile. Something *substantial*. I am trying hard not to be disappointed. To take pride in the work.

Charlotte and I wobble the wheelbarrow down a steeply sloped trail. The path opens into a large bog, rich with warm sunshine, surrounded by trees, dominated by a large shimmering pond. Spread all throughout the bog are small white cones protecting newly planted saplings.

The minute we enter the sunlight I am attacked by noise. Every atom of air seems to be screaming directly into my ears. There's a rising, falling, double-helixing tangle of sounds like a producer overdubbing a thousand tracks of locusts. Except, it's a hundred times louder and more intense than any locust I've ever heard. The sound ripples across my flesh. It is the feeling of wonder and joy, sensations I haven't felt in a long time.

Melanie says something and laughs, but I can't hear her. Once again, the sun has turned her glasses the color of smoke.

"What?" I shout.

"*Frogs*," she hollers.

This audio attack is the sound of frogs trying to find a mate. It makes me laugh, because all the chaos and confusion and overstimulation does kind of remind me of my recent foray into the world of dating apps. Swipe right, frogs. Swipe right.

"That's crazy!" I yell, but she probably doesn't hear me because she begins asking Charlotte where they should place the herp trap. This noise is no big deal to them; it's just part of their work environment. But I can't help but investigate. It's shocking how getting just ten feet closer to the pond amps up the decibels. I have something like tinnitus howling through my head and it knocks me a little off balance. I cannot see a single frog, so it's like these mating calls are bursting out from within the Earth itself.

I wander to the edge of the water and am captivated by a tree. At least I think it's a tree. It's skinny and leafless, but its trunk is a marvel of nature, about as thick as a firehose and festooned with massive spikes, like someone attached a series of shark's teeth into star patterns.

"That's a honey locust tree," Melanie says.

I've never had a favorite tree before, but I do now.

Hell, this might be my favorite place, period. Heavy metal death trees, frog calls that sound kind of like feedbacking Sonic Youth guitars, and now I'm part of a group helping rewild the Black Swamp? I love it. I never knew there were so many surprises in my old home. Wonders everywhere, hidden under the surface.

We begin digging a thin trench for our salamander fence. Charlotte carves a straight line with a spade, while I gouge away with a pickax. My arms burn and I'm sweating under that surprisingly strong March sunshine. A strong ache glows along my spine, and my boot bottoms are lumpy with caked-on black mud. My hands and pants are filthy with swamp dirt. Not, maybe, unlike my ancestor.

"Okay, stupid question," I say, letting go of pride. "Why exactly are we taking pictures of salamanders?"

"To see if they have a healthy population."

"What exactly does a healthy salamander population tell you?"

A healthy population means, essentially, that their rewilding efforts are working. Melanie proceeds to explain salamander life in passionate detail. Basically, a healthy salamander population says that there is clean water nearby, and it says that the water doesn't evaporate too quickly because of global warming. If the water is dirty or the sun zaps them too soon, salamander eggs die and the population dips significantly. If salamanders start fading, the animals who eat them fade, and the animals who eat those animals fade, domino after domino, so on and so on, all the way through the fragile ecological food chain. I am reminded of the similarly complex weave of the Toledo algae crisis. The complexity of my childhood. The complexity of my old married life and my new life, alone.

With invisible frogs boring a tunnel between my ears, I rest my hands on my head, breathing heavy. I'm exhausted. We get the long fence into place and rig up a solar-powered camera on each end. We're done. I'm still tickled by the call of a thousand bullfrogs and proud that my sweat has dripped onto the Great Black Swamp's soil. A part of me is now a part of the landscape. My hands and back hurt, my pants and feet and face are streaked with deep oil-colored mud, but I feel electric, basking in the satisfaction of reconnecting and creating something new in Northwest Ohio.

Maybe this is how Great-Great-Great-Grandfather felt upon conquering his corner of Henry County swamp? Maybe this is what reinvention feels like?

I carry this upbeat feeling with me as we pack up the wheelbarrow and lug it up the hill. It's been several hours, and we were all so focused we forgot to take a lunch break. They drop me off at my car and I lean against the fender, tugging off those muck boots and standing on hard gravel in my socks. I start hammering the hard rubber heels together. Dark scraps of mud fly in all directions. Filthy bits thump against my car, pepper my face, and fall to the ground in coagulated globs.

"I guess that'll have to be good enough," I say, seeing how impossible it will be to completely clean these boots.

"Looks like you're going to take a little of the Black Swamp home with you," Melanie laughs.

ACKNOWLEDGEMENTS

This book would not have been possible without the generous support of a Lincoln Memorial University mini-grant and an Appalachian College Association Faculty Fellowship. Thank you.

Thank you to Anne Trubek, whose enthusiasm, support, and guidance were crucial to this book.

Thank you to Phoebe Mogharei, whose sharp eye and wisdom helped me create the best version of this book possible.

Thank you to all the experts, people on the street, and others who spent time and energy speaking with me, many of whom did not make it into the final version of this book, unfortunately.

Thank you to my writing group, Kevin, Derrick, and Matt, for years of support and feedback, and love.

Thank you to my professors and cohort at the Portland State University MFA Program from 2017 to 2019. You had to sit through several really bad short stories about toxic algae and the Black Swamp before I realized nonfiction was the only way to tell this.

Thank you to my parents and my sister for letting me be such a weirdo as a child.

Most of all, thanks to my son, Walter. I love you.

BIBLIOGRAPHY

Aldrich, Lewis Cass. *History of Henry & Fulton Counties, with Illustrations & Biographical Sketches of Some of Its Prominent Men & Pioneers*. D. Mason & Co., 1888.

Allen, Greg. "A New Old Way to Combat Toxic Algae: Float It Up, Then Skim It Off." NPR, July 29, 2019. https://www.npr.org/2019/07/29/745666501/a-new-old-way-to-combat-toxic-algae-float-them-up-then-skim-them-off.

Allnut, Brian. "NOAA Layoffs Endanger Great Lakes, Experts Say: 'The Drivers Behind Keeping Us Safe.'" Planet Detroit, March 3, 2025. https://planetdetroit.org/2025/03/noaa-layoffs-impact-great-lakes/.

Almas, Michelle. "Black Swamp Meant Wilderness." *Sentinel Tribune*, August 7, 1970.

Amato, John. "Why Do We Say 'Holy Toledo'?: The History of Holy Toledo." Jūpmode. Accessed April 11, 2025. https://www.jupmode.com/blogs/news/holy-toledo.

Andrew, Scottie, and Melissa Gray. "A North Carolina Woman Took Her Three Dogs to a Pond to Play. Within Hours, Her Pups Had Died from Toxic Algae." CNN, August 12, 2019. https://www.cnn.com/2019/08/11/us/three-dogs-died-algae-trnd/index.html.

Aronoff, Kate. "Elon Musk's Doge Cuts Could Kill Your Dog." *The New Republic*, March 5, 2025. https://newrepublic.com/article/192346/musk-doge-noaa-water-safety-algae.

Azerrad, Michael. *Come As You Are*. Main Street Books, 1993.

Bain, Thomas D. "The Ecology and Vegetation of Goll's Woods." Master's thesis, Bowling Green State University, 1940.

Bannon, Christie. "'Toxic' Algae Alert at Beauty Spot." *Llanelli Star*, August 11, 2022.

Bathroom Readers'Institute, and William Dylan Powell. *Uncle John's Bathroom Reader Plunges into Ohio*. Printers Row Publishing Group, 2013.

Bennett, Laura. "Goll Woods in Archbold Spins Tall Tale of History." *Toledo Blade*, June 30, 2008.

Biello, David. "Deadly Algae Are Everywhere, Thanks to Agriculture." *Scientific American*, August 8, 2014.

The Blade. "Editorial: Let Algae Bloom." March 5, 2025. https://www.toledoblade.com/opinion/editorials/2025/03/05/editorial-let-algae-bloom-dont-slash-noaa-trump-government-cuts-ohio-michigan/stories/20%E2%80%A6.

Bloom, Matthew D. "Creating Connections: Economic Development, Land Use, and the System of Cities in Northwest Ohio During the Nineteenth Century." Dissertation, Bowling Green State University, 2009.

Boerner, Ralph E., and Do-Soon Cho. "Structure and Composition of Goll Woods, an Old-Growth Forest Remnant in Northwestern Ohio." *Bulletin of the Torrey Botanical Club* 114, no. 2 (April 1987): 173.

Bogart, Dana. "'My Great Terror, The Black Swamp': Northwest Ohio's Environmental Borderland." Master's thesis, Miami University, 2015.

Borer, Alan. "Buying Swamps, Selling Farms—Florien Giaque." *Salmagundi*, 2021. aborer1962.blogspot.com/2021/05/buying-swamp-selling-farms-florien.html.

Brady, Dennis, and Chris Mooney. "Neil Gorsuch's Mother Once Ran the EPA. It Didn't Go Well. Anne Gorsuch Slashed the EPA's Budget,

Scaled Back on Fighting Polluters and Alienated the Agency's Scientists During Her Short Tenure." *Washington Post*, February 1, 2017.

Bridge Michigan. "Michigan Farmers Using Too Much Fertilizer, Hurting Water Quality Efforts." Accessed April 28, 2025. https://www.bridgemi.com/michigan-environment-watch/michigan-farmers-using-too-much-fertilizer-hurting-water-quality-efforts.

Bruce, McGarvey. "Landscape Myths of the Black Swamp." *Northwest Ohio Quarterly* 60, no. 3 (1988).

Brzeziński, Bartosz. "Fertilizer Rescue Plan Brings No Relief to Europe's Farmers and Industry." Politico, November 10, 2022. https://www.politico.eu/article/fertilizer-rescue-plan-no-relief-europe-farmer-industry/.

Buckeye Steam Traction Ditcher. American Society of Mechanical Engineers, 1988.

Busch, Julius. "A Week in the Black Swamp." In *Travels Between the Hudson and the Mississippi: 1851–1852*, edited and translated by Norman H. Binger, University of Kentucky, 1971.

Business Week. "The Hard Job of Saving Lake Erie." October 27, 1975.

Buttrick, Tilly. *Buttrick's Voyages, Travels, and Discoveries, 1812–1819*. N.p., 1831.

Card, Nan. "Black Swamp Taverns." On file in the Rutherford B. Hayes Presidential Library, n.d. Accessed 2025.

———. "Rose Tavern." On file in the Rutherford B. Hayes Presidential Library, n.d. Accessed 2025.

Carmichael, Wayne W., Sandra M. Azevedo, Ji Si An, Renato J. Molica, Elise M. Jochimsen, Sharon Lau, Kenneth L. Rinehart, Glen R. Shaw and Geoff K. Eaglesham. "Human Fatalities from Cyanobacteria: Chemical and Biological Evidence for Cyanotoxins." *Environmental Health Perspectives* 109, no. 7 (July 2001): 663.

Carroll, Sean B. *The Serengeti Rules: The Quest to Discover How Life Works and Why It Matters*. Princeton University Press, 2024.

Casado, Freixys. "When in Doubt, Stay Out: Nevada's Drought Could Worsen Outbreaks of Toxic Algae." Kolo 8 News Now, July 6, 2022.

https://www.kolotv.com/2022/07/06/when-doubt-stay-out-nevadas-drought-could-worsen-outbreaks-toxic-algae/.

Chanatry, Hannah. "Woods Hole Report Identifies Concerns, Possible Solutions for Harmful Algae Blooms." WBUR News, January 15, 2022. https://www.wbur.org/news/2022/01/15/toxic-algae-report-woods-hole.

Chang, Ruth. "Trailblazers of the Great Black Swamp: 31 Miles, 31 Taverns." Midstory, December 28, 2023. https://www.midstory.org/trailblazers-of-the-great-black-swamp-31-miles-31-taverns/.

Chicago Tribune. "Dillinger Gang's Buried Loot Still an Alluring Legend." August 8, 2021. https://www.chicagotribune.com/1988/02/23/dillinger-gangs-buried-loot-still-an-alluring-legend/.

The Conversation. "Climate Change Is Causing Algal Blooms in Lake Superior for the First Time in History." April 16, 2025. https://theconversation.com/climate-change-is-causing-algal-blooms-in-lake-superior-for-the-first-time-in-history-233515.

Crop Economics for Ohio. Ohio State University, 1962.

Daley, Jason. "Toledo, Ohio, Just Granted Lake Erie the Same Legal Rights as People." *Smithsonian Magazine*, March 1, 2019. https://www.smithsonianmag.com/smart-news/toledo-ohio-just-granted-lake-erie-same-legal-rights-people-180971603/.

Daly, Matthew. "EPA Plans to Cut Scientific Research Program, Could Fire More than 1,000 Employees." AP News, March 18, 2025. https://apnews.com/article/epa-science-layoffs-trump-doge-8a5743b9281e3f82afdf2cdd5f972d5f.

Dangler, Prudence. *A Brief History of Deshler*. Deshler Chamber of Commerce, 1954.

Danoff, Bill. "A Journey Down a Country Road; John Denver's Songs Traveled with a Smile." *Washington Post*, October 14, 1997.

Democratic Northwest. "Notice to Non-Resident Land Owners." May 28, 1896.

Dempsey, David. "Picture of a Small Town in the Atomic Age." *New York Times*, June 5, 1949.

"Deshler Land Company Info." A series of letters in the Bowling Green State University Jerome Library Archives, n.d. Accessed 2025.

Deshler, Ohio, 1876–1976: A Historical Collection. Deshler Chamber of Commerce, 1976.

Dickens, Charles, and Patricia Ingham. *American Notes*. Penguin Books, 2004.

Dorsey, David. "Following Fertilizer Leads to Farms, Golf Courses, Landscaping amid Algae Blooms." *Naples Daily News*, September 21, 2018. https://www.naplesnews.com/story/news/environment/2018/09/21/florida-algae-crisis-following-fertilizer-leads-farms-golf-courses-landscaping/1377916002/.

Downes, Randolph. "The Black Swamp of Ohio." *Buckeye Historian*, 1960.

Economic Research Service. "Corn and Other Feed Grains—Feed Grains Sector at a Glance." Accessed May 26, 2025. https://www.ers.usda.gov/topics/crops/corn-and-other-feed-grains/feed-grains-sector-at-a-glance.

Egan, Dan. *The Death and Life of the Great Lakes*. W.W. Norton & Company, 2018.

———. *The Devil's Element: Phosphorus and a World Out of Balance*. W.W. Norton & Company, 2024.

Ellzey, Bill. "Raceland Farmer Invented Digging Machines." Houma Today, February 25, 2018. https://www.houmatoday.com/story/lifestyle/around-town/2018/02/25/photographs-and-memories-raceland-farmer-invented-digging-machines/14127969007/.

Endres, David J. "What Medicine Could Not Cure: Faith Healings at the Shrine of Our Lady of Consolation, Carey, Ohio." *U.S. Catholic Historian* 34, no. 3 (2016): 25–49.

Environmental Working Group. "Manure from Unregulated Factory Farms Fuels Lake Erie's Toxic Algae Blooms." Accessed April 28, 2025. https://www.ewg.org/news-insights/news/manure-unregulated-factory-farms-fuels-lake-eries-toxic-algae-blooms.

———. "Nitrogen Fertilizer's Toll: Not Just Dead Zones." Accessed April 28, 2025. https://www.ewg.org/news-insights/news/nitrogen-fertilizers-toll-not-just-dead-zones.

Erb, Robin. "Toledo Drinking-Water Ban Lifted, but Residents Wary." *USA Today*, August 4, 2014.

Evers, C.W., and F.J. Oblinger. *Many Incidents and Reminiscences of the Early History of Wood County: Together with Some of the Historic Events of the Maumee Valley Contained in This Pioneer Scrap-book, Have Been Collected from the Papers and Material of the Late C.W. Evers as Gathered by Him for Years Past*. Heritage Books, 2002.

Faber, Don. *The Toledo War: The First Michigan-Ohio Rivalry*. University of Michigan Press, 2008.

Fackler, Eliot. "Domesticating to Country: Indigenous Power and Colonialism in the Black Swamp of the Old Northwest." PhD diss., University of Illinois at Chicago, 2020.

Fang, Lee. "Lobbying Blitz Pushed Fertilizer Prices Higher, Fueling Food Inflation." The Intercept, August 3, 2022. https://theintercept.com/2022/08/03/fertilizer-prices-food-inflation-mosaic/.

Farr, Jamie, and Robert Blair Kaiser. *Just Farr Fun*. Eubanks/Donizetti, 1994.

Fawcett-Atkinson, Marc. "Dog Photos and Veiled Threats: How Canada's Fertilizer Lobby Is Fighting Against Climate Laws." Canada's National Observer, November 20, 2022. https://www.nationalobserver.com/2022/07/04/investigations/how-canadas-fertilizer-lobby-fighting-climate-laws.

Ferdman, Roberto. "How Corn Made Its Way into Just About Everything We Eat." *Washington Post*, July 14, 2015.

Fertilizer Use and Price Statistics, 1960–88. U.S. Economic Research Service, 1989.

Figueroa, Fernando, and Serra Sowers/WUFT News. "Critics Warn Against Industry-Driven Environmental Research Agendas in Florida." *Columbia Missourian*, June 2, 2023. https://www.columbiamissourian.

com/priceofplenty/elements/critics-warn-against-industry-driven-environmental-research-agendas-in-florida/article_995128f0-00e8-11ee-8c0f-4f57176b4019.html.

FitzGerald, Emmett. "For the Love of Peat." 99% Invisible, July 6, 2021. https://99percentinvisible.org/episode/for-the-love-of-peat/transcript/.

Fleischman, John. "Heart of Flatness." *Ohio Magazine*, October 1994.

Floyd, Barbara. *Legendary Locals of Toledo, Ohio*. The History Press, 2016.

Frankel, Todd. "The Toxin That Shut Off Toledo's Water? The Feds Don't Make You Test for It." *Washington Post*, August 11, 2014.

Gearhart, Tom. "Ditty Gets Dander Up of Men Strong for Toledo." *Toledo Blade*, March 25, 1973.

———. "Saturday in Toledo Busy for Denver." *Toledo Blade*, November 11, 1973.

Gilbert, Mike. "The Black Swamp." Hayes Presidential Library. Speech, October 31, 2015.

Gilinsky, Victor. "Heard About the Near-Accident at the Ohio Nuclear Plant? I'm Not Surprised." *Washington Post*, April 27, 2002.

Gilmartin, Dave. *The Absolutely Worst Places to Live in America*. St. Martin's Griffin, 2015.

Glueck, Grace. "David Dempsey, 85, a Writer On Wide-Ranging Subjects." *New York Times*, January 19, 1999.

Good, Howard E. *Black Swamp Farm*. Ohio State University Press, 1997.

Gorman, Julia. "Former Employee: 20% of Ann Arbor NOAA Office Cut, Community to Feel Impacts." 13 On Your Side, February 27, 2025. https://www.wzzm13.com/article/news/local/former-employee-20-ann-arbor-noaa-office-cut-community-to-feel-impacts/69-6ad17acd-9758-43c2-b98f-aa65707d7a14.

The Great Black Swamp: The Indian Wars. Great Black Swamp Games (a Junior Achievement Co.), 1983.

Greene, Bob. "Joe the Plumber, Meet Vicki Cole." CNN, October 16, 2008. https://politicalticker.blogs.cnn.com/2008/10/16/greene-joe-the-plumber-meet-vicki-cole/.

The Guardian. "'Chaos': Trump Cuts to NOAA Disrupt Staffing and Weather Forecasts." April 1, 2025. https://www.theguardian.com/us-news/2025/apr/01/trump-cuts-noaa-spam-emails.

Hallegraeff, Gustaaf M., Donald M. Anderson, Catherine Belin, Marie-Yasmine Dechraoui Bottein, Eileen Bresnan, Mireille Chinain, Henrik Enevoldsen, et al. "Perceived Global Increase in Algal Blooms Is Attributable to Intensified Monitoring and Emerging Bloom Impacts." Nature News, June 8, 2021. https://www.nature.com/articles/s43247-021-00178-8.

Hance, Jeremy. "Lethal Algae Blooms—An Ecosystem Out of Balance." *The Guardian*, January 4, 2020. https://www.theguardian.com/environment/2020/jan/04/lethal-algae-blooms-an-ecosystem-out-of-balance.

Hart, Nathan. "Presidents, Moonwalkers and Actors: Who Are the Famous People from Ohio's 88 Counties?" *Columbus Dispatch*, March 30, 2024. https://www.dispatch.com/story/news/2024/03/30/here-are-the-most-famous-people-from-each-of-ohios-88-counties/72867817007/.

Harvey, Chelsea. "Algal Blooms Have Boomed Worldwide." *Scientific American*, February 20, 2024. https://www.scientificamerican.com/article/algal-blooms-have-boomed-worldwide/.

Hawley, Steven Anthony. "Black Swamp Babies: An Historical Analysis of Family and Fertility in Northwest Ohio, 1830–1860." PhD diss., Bowling Green State University, 1989.

Henry County, Ohio, Families. "Brief History of the Founding of Bartlow Township in Early 1850s." November 18, 2016. https://henrycountyfamilies.org/index.php/category/county-history/.

Henry, Tom. "Algal Blooms Will Likely Be Around for a Long Time." *The Blade*, September 4, 2024. https://www.toledoblade.com/local/environment/2024/09/04/algal-blooms-future-western-lake-erie-toxic-algae-science-conference-stranahan/stories/20240904156.

———. "Former NOAA Administrator Says the Great Lakes Region Will Feel Impact of Layoffs." *The Blade*, March 2, 2025. https://www.toledoblade.com/local/environment/2025/03/02/former-noaa-administrator-says-great-lakes-region-feel-impact-layoffs/stories/20250302085.

———. "International Algae Conference Opens at BGSU." *Toledo Blade*, April 14, 2015.

———. "Toxic Algae Struggles Leave Toledo's Reputation Hanging in the Balance." *Toledo Blade*, August 2, 2015.

Herdendor, Charles. "Understanding Lake Erie's Pollution Problems." *Ohio Woodlands* (Spring 1978).

Hill, James B. "Untitled Autobiography." Hancock County Historical Society, Findlay, Ohio.

Hinds, Conrade C. *Made in Ohio: A History of Buckeye Invention and Ingenuity*. The History Press, 2023.

Howe, Henry. *Howe's Historical Collections of Ohio in Two Volumes: An Encyclopedia of the State*. State of Ohio, 1898.

Howes, Laura. "What Happens When the Water in Our Rivers and Lakes Reaches Record Lows?" Chemical & Engineering News, March 25, 2023. https://cen.acs.org/environment/climate-change/happens-water-rivers-lakes-reaches/100/i38.

Hullinger, Jessica. "How a Tiny Utah Town Eliminated Toxic Algal Blooms in Its Reservoir." Fast Company, June 25, 2024. https://www.fastcompany.com/91145726/utah-toxic-algal-blooms-lakeguard-oxy.

Huma Gro. "10 Fertilizer Facts for Global Fertilizer Day 2022." Accessed April 25, 2025. https://humagro.com/10-fertilizer-facts-for-global-fertilizer-day-2022/.

Illman, Harry R. *Unholy Toledo*. Commonwealth Book Company, 2023.

The Independent. "Toxic Algae on Windermere Is a Sign of What's to Come." August 22, 2022.

Irwin, R.W. *Review of Land Drainage in Ontario*. Ontario Agricultural College, 1962.

Jeffay, John. "Toxic Algae May Be Killing Seabirds Washed Up on Shore." *The Times*, October 12, 2021.

Jepson, Paul, and Cain Blythe. *Rewilding: The Radical New Science of Ecological Recovery*. MIT Press, 2022.

Jones, J. Brenton. "Plant Analysis." In *Ohio Report on Research and Development*, April 1965.

Kaatz, Martin R. "The Black Swamp: A Study in Historical Geography." *Annals of the Association of American Geographers* 45, no. 1 (March 1955): 1–35.

Kaatz, Martin. "The Settlement of the Black Swamp of Northwest Ohio: Early Days." *Northwest Ohio Quarterly*, 1952.

Kahn, Joseph. "In China, a Lake's Champion Imperils Himself." *New York Times*, June 1, 1980.

Karr, James R., Louis A. Toth, and Daniel R. Dudley. "Fish Communities of Midwestern Rivers: A History of Degradation." *BioScience* 35, no. 2 (February 1985): 90–95.

Keiffer, Artimus. *The Geography of Ohio*. Kent State University Press, 2008.

Keller, Kathryn, and Gordon Keller. "The Worst Road in the Country." *Toledo Blade*, September 18, 1966.

Kemp, Adam. "As NOAA Braces for More Cuts, Scientists Say Public Safety Is at Risk." PBS, March 14, 2025. https://www.pbs.org/newshour/nation/as-noaa-braces-for-more-cuts-scientists-say-public-safety-is-at-risk.

Klein, Robert. "Provenance of a Ditcher." Letter to Sue Tucker, director of the Hancock County Historical Museum, Findlay, Ohio, February 2000. Accessed 2025.

Kleinman, Peter J., Andrew N. Sharpley, Paul J. Withers, Lars Bergström, Laura T. Johnson and Donnacha G. Doody. "Implementing Agricultural Phosphorus Science and Management to Combat Eutrophication." *Ambio* 44, no. 2 (February 15, 2015): 297–310.

Kluger, Jeffrey. "The True Cost of Trump's Cuts to NOAA and NASA." *Time*, March 13, 2025. https://time.com/7267889/climate-cost-of-trump-staff-cuts-noaa-nasa/.

Kool, Nancy. "Deserting the Great Lakes." *Cleveland Magazine*, November 1981.

Kosta, Michael. "The Fight to Turn Lake Erie Into a Person." YouTube. Accessed April 30, 2025. https://www.youtube.com/watch?v=3fyUD28UtlU&ab_channel=TheDailyShow.

Kraft, Amy. "Algae Bloom Toxin Linked to Alzheimer's, Other Diseases." CBS News, January 22, 2016. https://www.cbsnews.com/news/algae-bloom-toxin-linked-to-alzheimers-and-other-neurodegenerative-diseases/.

Kuron, Frank E. *Sketches of Intriguing People: And the Curious Events They Suffered While Living in the Wilderness of the Northwest Territory*. Kuron Publishing, 2020.

Larsen, David P., Daniel R. Dudley and Robert M. Hughes. "A Regional Approach for Assessing Attainable Surface Water Quality: An Ohio Case Study." *Journal of Soil and Water Conservation* 43, no. 2 (March 1988): 171–76.

Lauck, Jon. *The Good Country: A History of the American Midwest, 1800–1900*. University of Oklahoma Press, 2022.

Levy, Sharon. *The Marsh Builders: The Fight for Clean Water, Wetlands, and Wildlife*. Oxford University Press, 2020.

Licon, Adriana Gomez. "Musk Waves a Chainsaw and Charms Conservatives Talking Up Trump's Cost-Cutting Efforts." AP News, February 21, 2025. https://apnews.com/article/musk-chainsaw-trump-doge-6568e9e0cfc42ad6cdcfd58a409eb312.

Lim, Kay. "Remembering the Great Toilet Paper Shortage of 1973." CBS News, April 5, 2020. https://www.cbsnews.com/news/remembering-the-great-toilet-paper-shortage-of-1973/.

Lintelman, Ryan. "In 1968, When Nixon Said 'Sock It to Me' on 'Laugh-in,' TV Was Never Quite the Same Again." *Smithsonian Magazine*,

January 19, 2018. https://www.smithsonianmag.com/smithsonian-institution/1968-when-nixon-said-sock-it-me-laugh-tv-was-never-quite-same-again-180967869/.

"Liver Failure and Death After Exposure to Microcystins at a Hemodialysis Center in Brazil." *New England Journal of Medicine* 339, no. 2 (July 9, 1998): 873–78.

Long, Tedd, Stephanie Delo and Yarko Kuk. *Forgotten Visitors: Northwest Ohio's Notable Guests*. University of Toledo Press, 2020.

Lydecker, Ryck. "The Death and Rebirth of Lake Erie." *Nautical Quarterly* 37 (1987).

Magas, Nicole. "Exclusive: Fertilizer Lobby 'Trying to Scare Farmers' to Head Off Reductions in Climate Super-Pollutant." The Energy Mix, November 20, 2024. https://www.theenergymix.com/2021/10/19/exclusive-fertilizer-lobby-trying-to-scare-farmers-to-head-off-reductions-in-climate-super-pollutant/.

Malcolm, Jess. "Toxic Algae Alert for Murray-Darling." *The Australian*, February 4, 2021.

Malcolm, M.A. Mimi. *The Firebugs of Northwest Ohio*. N.p., 2016.

Mann, Barbara Alice. *Land of the Three Miamis: A Traditional Narrative of the Iroquois in Ohio*. Urban Affairs Center Press, 2009.

Manning, Richard. *Against the Grain: How Agriculture Has Hijacked Civilization*. North Point Press, 2004.

Martin, Sandi. "UGA Researchers Identify, Name Toxic Cyanobacteria Killing American Bald Eagles." UGA Today, December 12, 2017. https://news.uga.edu/identify-name-toxic-cyanobacteria-killing-american-bald-eagles-0215/.

Mauk, Clint, and Tom Walton. *Historical Tales of Toledo*. Woodlands Publishing, 2004.

Maynard, Kevin. *History of Evansport*. Stryker Area Heritage Council, 2010.

Mays, Chris, Vivi Vajda and Stephen McLoughlin. "Toxic Slime Contributed to Earth's Worst Mass Extinction—and It's Making a

Comeback." *Scientific American*, February 20, 2024. https://www.scientificamerican.com/article/toxic-slime-contributed-to-earth-rsquo-s-worst-mass-extinction-mdash-and-it-rsquo-s-making-a-comeback/.

McKie, Robin. "Misuse of Phosphorus Is Wreaking Havoc, Scientists Warn." Mother Jones, March 14, 2023. https://www.motherjones.com/environment/2023/03/phosphorus-fertilizer-shortage-algae-dead-zones-environment-runoff/.

McNutt, Randy. *Lost Ohio: More Travels into the Haunted Landscapes, Ghost Towns, and Forgotten Lives*. Kent State University Press, 2012.

McPhee, John. *The Control of Nature*. Farrar, Straus and Giroux, 2011.

Michigan in the World. "Give Earth a Chance: Environmental Activism in Michigan." Accessed April 9, 2025. https://michigenintheworld.history.lsa.umich.edu/environmentalism.

Miller, Kimberly. "Toxic Algae Closes Palm Beach County Floodcontrol Structure." *Palm Beach Post*, May 20, 2021.

Miller, Larry L. *Ohio Place Names*. Indiana University Press, 1996.

Milman, Olivia. "'Chaos': Trump Cuts to NOAA Disrupt Staffing and Weather Forecasts." *The Guardian*, April 1, 2025. https://www.theguardian.com/us-news/2025/apr/01/trump-cuts-noaa-spam-emails.

Minder, Raphael. "'Green Soup' Engulfs a Pristine Mediterranean Lagoon." *New York Times*, October 18, 2021.

Modlin, Daniel. "The Dog-Killing Bacteria Plaguing a Popular National Park." The Daily Beast, September 8, 2024. https://www.thedailybeast.com/the-mysterious-dog-killing-bacteria-plaguing-a-popular-national-park/.

Mollenkopf, Jim. *The Great Black Swamp: Historical Tales of 19th-Century Northwest Ohio*. Lake of the Cat Pub, 1999.

———. *The Great Black Swamp III: Further Historical Tales of Northwestern Ohio*. Lake of the Cat Pub, 2008.

Monbiot, George. *Feral: Rewilding the Land, Sea, and Human Life*. Penguin Books, 2014.

Napier, Hooks, Kohl and Hansen. "Rural Life and Farmer Attitudes: An Ohio Survey." *Research Circular*, October 1980.

NASA. "Greening the Gulf of Finland." Accessed April 28, 2025. https://earthobservatory.nasa.gov/images/150197/greening-the-gulf-of-finland.

National Agricultural Law Center. "Turning the Tides: Judge Finds Lake Erie Bill of Rights Unconstitutional." Accessed April 30, 2025. https://nationalaglawcenter.org/turning-the-tides-judge-finds-lake-erie-bill-of-rights-unconstitutional/.

National Archives and Records Administration. "Vietnam War U.S. Military Fatal Casualty Statistics." Accessed April 25, 2025. https://www.archives.gov/research/military/vietnam-war/casualty-statistics.

National Railroad Hall of Fame. "Whistlestop Campaigning." Accessed April 9, 2025. https://www.nrrhof.org/whistlestop.

Neupane, Ghanashyam, and Sheila J. Roberts. "Quantitative Comparison of Heavy Metals and as Accumulation in Agricultural and Forest Soils near Bowling Green, Ohio." *Water, Air, and Soil Pollution* 197, nos. 1–4 (August 13, 2008): 289–301.

New Bremen Historic Association. "The Great Black Swamp." Accessed April 25, 2025. https://newbremenhistory.org/en/content/70-the-great-black-swamp.

Nguyen, Tien. "Reviving a Famously Polluted California Lake." *Knowable Magazine*, August 9, 2023. https://knowablemagazine.org/content/article/food-environment/2023/reviving-famously-polluted-california-lake.

Nicco, Mike, and Tim Didion. "Environmental Groups Push for Increased River Flow in Wake of Toxic Algal Bloom in Delta Waterways." ABC7 San Francisco, October 27, 2022. https://abc7news.com/san-joaquin-delta-algae-bloom-toxic-algal-francisco-bay/12382084/.

Nugent, Ciara. "How One Environmental Activist Is Taking on India's Pollution Problem." *Time*, October 13, 2022. https://time.com/6218247/arun-krishnamurthy-2/.

Ohio Agriculture. June 1967.

OpenSecrets. "Fertilizer Institute Lobbying Profile." Accessed April 28, 2025. https://www.opensecrets.org/federal-lobbying/clients/summary?cycle=2021&id=D000025789.

O'Rourke, P.J. "P. J. O'Rourke Reflects on Toledo, His Hometown." *Newsweek*, September 14, 2011. https://www.newsweek.com/p-j-orourke-reflects-toledo-his-hometown-66161.

Owens, Jack. "A Long-Overdue Evaluation of Benjamin Hough's Observation for Latitude of the North Cape of Maumee Bay, Ohio's Northern Border." *Michigan Historical Review* 44, no. 2 (September 2018): 97–124.

PBS. "The Story of the Great Black Swamp." 1982. https://www.pbs.org/video/wbgu-documentaries-the-story-of-the-great-black-swamp/.

PBS NewsHour. "How Drones Could Limit Fertilizer Flow into Lake Erie." September 10, 2014. https://www.pbs.org/newshour/show/using-drones-limit-fertilizer-flow-lake-erie.

Pennisi, Elizabeth. "To Tame Lake-Fouling Algal Blooms, Try an Ecosystem Approach." Science, July 6, 2022. https://www.science.org/content/article/to-tame-lake-fouling-algal-blooms-try-an-ecosystem-approach.

Perkins, Frank. "Buckeye Traction Ditcher." *Scientific American*, September 4, 1904.

Perry, Alex. "Are 'Ohio' Memes the Source of 'Brainrot' Among Gen Alpha? Here's What We Know." *Enquirer*, August 15, 2024. https://www.cincinnati.com/story/news/2024/08/15/ohio-meme-gen-alpha-what-it-means-taking-over-internet/74769457007/.

Peters, Adele. "Trump Plans to Slash Jobs at NOAA. That Could Make It Riskier to Fly." Fast Company, February 26, 2025. https://www.fastcompany.com/91284862/trump-plans-to-slash-jobs-at-noaa-that-could-make-it-riskier-to-fly.

Peters, Hammerson. "The Adventures of Rene-Robert Cavelier, Sieur de La Salle." Mysteries of Canada, November 11, 2021. https://mysteriesofcanada.com/quebec/the-adventures-of-rene-robert-cavelier-sieur-de-la-salle/.

Pouria, Shideh, A. de Andrade, J. Barbosa, R.L. Cavalcanti, V.T.S. Barreto, C.J. Ward, W. Preiser, Grace K. Poon, G.H. Neild, and G.A. Codd. "Fatal Microcystin Intoxication in Haemodialysis Unit in Caruaru, Brazil." *The Lancet* 352, no. 9121 (July 1998): 21–26.

Proulx, Annie. *Fen, Bog and Swamp: A Short History of Peatland Destruction and Its Role in the Climate Crisis*. Scribner, 2023.

Putnam, G.W. "Four Months with Charles Dickens." *The Atlantic*, November 1, 1870. https://www.theatlantic.com/magazine/archive/1870/11/four-months-with-charles-dickens/306681/.

Ohio Agriculture Statistics 1949 and 1950. Ohio Agriculture Experiment Station, 1951.

Ohio Agriculture Statistics 1953 and 1954. Ohio Agriculture Experiment Station, 1955.

Ohio Agriculture Statistics 1957 and 1958. Ohio Agriculture Experiment Station, 1959.

Ohio Agriculture Statistics 1965–70. Ohio Agriculture Experiment Station, 1971.

Ohio Agriculture Statistics 1980–83. Ohio Agriculture Experiment Station, 1986.

Ohio State Office of Research. "Robert Fenton, Electrical and Computer Engineering." November 13, 2019. https://research.osu.edu/robert-fenton.

Reuters. "Brazil's Fertilizer Lobby Pledges $4 Billion Outlay to Cut Import Dependence." March 9, 2023. https://www.reuters.com/article/brazil-fertilizer/brazils-fertilizer-lobby-pledges-4-billion-outlay-to-cut-import-dependence-idUSL1N35H281/.

———. "Factbox: What Could Be Causing Botswana's Mystery Elephant Deaths?"Accessed April 28, 2025. https://www.reuters.com/article/us-botswana-elephants-theories-factbox-idUSKBN2441IV.

———. "What Could Be Causing Botswana's Mystery Elephant Deaths?" September 29, 2020. https://www.reuters.com/article/us-botswana-elephants-theories-factbox-idUSKBN2441IV.

Richards, R. Peter, Frank G. Calhoun and Gerald Matisoff. "The Lake Erie Agricultural Systems for Environmental Quality Project." *Journal of Environmental Quality* 31, no. 1 (January 2002): 6–16.

Ries, Julia. "Intense Heat Is Triggering Toxic Algae. Here's What to Know Before You Swim." Outside Online, August 9, 2024. https://www.outsideonline.com/health/wellness/harmful-algal-blooms-health-effects/.

Rosenbaum, Margo. "Deadly Algal Bloom Could Cause Food Shortage for Bay Area Migrating Waterbirds." Audubon, September 5, 2024. https://www.audubon.org/news/deadly-algal-bloom-could-cause-food-shortage-bay-area-migrating-waterbirds.

Russel, Darrell A., and Gerald G. Williams. "History of Chemical Fertilizer Development." *Soil Science Society of America Journal* 41, no. 2 (March 1977): 260–65.

Safire, William. "Fired Up: On Language." *New York Times*, January 20, 2008.

Samuel, Sigal. "Lake Erie Now Has Legal Rights, Just like You." Vox, February 26, 2019. https://www.vox.com/future-perfect/2019/2/26/18241904/lake-erie-legal-rights-personhood-nature-environment-toledo-ohio.

Save Barnegat Bay. "NJ's 2011 Fertilizer Law—Protecting Barnegat Bay, Restoring Its Ecosystem." Accessed April 28, 2025. https://savebarnegatbay.org/initiative/njs-2011-fertilizer-law/.

Schnurr, Ryan. *In the Watershed: A Journey Down the Maumee River*. Belt Publishing, 2017.

Scott, J.W. *A Presentation of Causes Tending to Fix the Position of the Future Great City of the World in the Central Plain of North America: Showing That the Centre of the World's Commerce, Now Represented by the City of London, Is Moving Westward to the City of New York, and Thence Within One Hundred Years, to the Best Position on the Great Lakes*. Blade Steam Book and Job Print, 1868.

Seckel, Scott. "Algae Bloom May Be Behind Mysterious California Deaths." Phys.org, June 20, 2023. https://phys.org/news/2021-08-algae-bloom-mysterious-california-deaths.html.

Seewer, John. "Toledo, Ohio: Don't Drink Tap Water." *Telegraph Herald*, August 2, 2014.

Sentinel Tribune. "BGSU Research Finds Reduced Levels of Harmful Algae Toxins in Sandusky Bay." September 3, 2024. https://www.sent-trib.com/2024/09/03/bgsu-research-finds-reduced-levels-of-harmful-algae-toxins-in-sandusky-bay/.

Simonis, Louis A., and William C. Holgate. *Maumee River, 1835: With the William C. Holgate Journal, May 16–June 24, 1835, from Utica, New York, to Huntington, Indiana*. Riverview Press, 2021.

Spectrum News. "Harmful Algal Bloom Underway in Lake Erie." Accessed April 11, 2025. https://spectrumnews1.com/oh/columbus/weather/2023/08/08/harmful-algal-bloom-underway-in-lake-erie.

Spokesman Review. "Toledo Toasts the End of Tainted Tap Water." 2014.

Swenson, Kyle. "'Make Chicago Safe Again': Giuliani Blames Democrats for City's Crime After 63 Shot Over Weekend." *Washington Post*, August 6, 2018.

Taylor, Richard. *Girty*. University Press of Kentucky, 2022.

Tercek, Katie. "'Lake Erie Is Not a Toilet': Tons of Animal Waste Is Washing into the Water, Expert Says." https://www.cleveland19.com, August 11, 2021. https://www.cleveland19.com/2021/08/11/lake-erie-is-not-toilet-tons-animal-waste-is-washing-into-water-expert-says/.

Time. "Nation: Toward the Nixon Inauguration." January 17, 1969. https://time.com/archive/6632942/nation-toward-the-nixon-inauguration/.

Times Picayune. "Grandpa of Tanks Ponders on War." N.d.

Toledo Blade. "'Saturday Night' Ditty Tells It Like It Is." April 4, 1973.

UPI. "It's Been 16 Years Since Vicki Lynn Cole Became." October 10, 1984. https://www.upi.com/Archives/1984/10/10/Its-been-16-years-since-Vicki-Lynn-Cole-became/6715466228800/.

———. "Minister's Daughter Gives Nixon Theme for His Administration." November 7, 1968.

Viviano, Joanne. "Shrine of Our Lady Offers Hope to Pilgrims in Northwestern Ohio." *Columbus Dispatch*, August 6, 2015.

Volk, G.W., and L.D. Baver. "Phosphorus Pollution of Lake Erie." *Ohio Report on Research and Development*, September 1970.

Walker, Samuel. "The Utah Lake Restoration Project Moves Forward as the Public Remains Divided." Utah Business, October 11, 2024. https://www.utahbusiness.com/archive/2022/10/28/utah-lake-restoration-project-begins-construction/.

Walton, Brett. "Marine Blooms of Harmful Algae Increasing in Europe, Much of the Americas." Circle of Blue, March 10, 2025. https://www.circleofblue.org/2021/world/marine-blooms-of-harmful-algae-increasing-in-europe-much-of-the-americas/.

Wangrin, Charlotte. Pete Wilhelm, Oral History. Other. Henry County Historical Society, March 20, 2010.

Wendler, Marilyn Van Voorhis. *The Foot of the Rapids: The Biography of a River Town: Maumee, Ohio, 1838–1988*. Daring Books, 1988.

Wiedemeier, Hannah. "How Corn Production's Change over Time Impacts Products." Nebraska Corn Board, November 30, 2022. https://nebraskacorn.gov/cornstalk/corn101/how-corn-productions-change-over-time-impacts-products/.

Wilhelm, Pete. "When Tile Came to the Black Swamp It Was Like Pulling the Plug." *Farmland News*, May 1985.

Wilhelm, Peter. "Draining the Black Swamp." *Northwest Ohio Quarterly* (Summer 1984).

Williams, Lindsey. *Arise Wild Land: As We Were in Milton Township, Ohio*. Atkinson Printing, 1982.

Williams, Rebecca. "Green Goo Growing in Lake Erie Is Not What You Think It Is." Michigan Public, November 12, 2015. https://www.michiganpublic.org/environment-science/2014-08-28/green-goo-growing-in-lake-erie-is-not-what-you-think-it-is.

Williams, Timothy. "Legal Rights for Lake Erie? Voters in Ohio City Will Decide." *New York Times*, February 18, 2019.

Winegard, Timothy C. *The Mosquito: A Human History of Our Deadliest Predator*. Penguin Random House, 2020.

Wines, Michael. "Behind Toledo's Water Crisis, a Long-Troubled Lake Erie." *New York Times*, August 5, 2014.

Winter, Nevin O. *A History of Northwest Ohio: A Narrative Account of Its Historical Progress and Development from...the First European Exploration of the Maumee and Sandusky Valleys and the Adjacent Shores of Lake Erie, Down to the Present Time*. Hardpress Ltd., 2013.

WUFT. "The Price of Plenty." June 5, 2023. https://projects.wuft.org/priceofplenty/.

WUSF. "The Price of Plenty: Digging into the Dirt." June 8, 2023. https://www.wusf.org/environment/2023-06-08/the-price-of-plenty-digging-into-the-dirt.

Yeoman, Barry. "The Algae That (Almost) Ate Toledo." Natural Resources Defense Council, July 27, 2015. https://www.nrdc.org/stories/algae-almost-ate-toledo.

Yourist, Leonard. "Deshler Citizens Blushing Under National Gaze." *Toledo Blade*, November 8, 1968.

Yousef, Yousef. "Why We Need to Fix the World's Freshwater Algal Bloom Problem." World Economic Forum, September 29, 2022. https://www.weforum.org/agenda/2022/09/freshwater-lakes-toxic-algal-bloom/.

ABOUT THE AUTHOR

Patrick Wensink the author of five books, including the bestseller *Broken Piano for President*. He is also the author of two books for children. His journalism appears in *The New York Times*, *Esquire*, *Salon*, *Men's Health*, *Oxford American*, and others. He is a professor of creative writing and directs the Mountain Heritage Literary Festival at Lincoln Memorial University. He was born and raised in Deshler, Ohio. *The New Yorker* once wrote one whole sentence about him.

Belt Publishing

beltpublishing.com